378·1

D1179076

This book is to be ret....... before
the last date stamped below.

2/4792

TERTIARY

*A radical approach to
post-compulsory education*

Edited by

A. B. Cotterell & E. W. Heley

Stanley Thornes (Publishers) Ltd.

First published in 1981 by Stanley Thornes (Publishers) Ltd., Educa House, Liddington Estate, Leckhampton Road, Cheltenham, Glos, GL53 0DN

British Library Cataloguing in Publication Data

Cotterell, Arthur B
    Tertiary
    1. Education, Secondary – Great Britain – History – 20th century
    2. Twelfth grade (Education) – History – 20th century
    3. Vocational education – Great Britain – History – 20th century
    I. Title   II Heley, Eric W
    373.2'38'0941   LA635

    ISBN   0 85950 402 6

Typeset by Buckway Printing Co. Ltd., Cirencester
Printed in England by The Pitman Press, Bath

CONTENTS

Notes are given at the end of each essay.

LIST OF CONTRIBUTORS

J. W. Ballard
Principal of Richmond upon Thames College. Formerly Vice-Principal of Yeovil College.

A. B. Cotterell
Assistant Principal (Students) at Richmond upon Thames College. Formerly Head of Department of Adult Education, North Herts College.

E. W. Heley
Assistant Principal (Academic) at Richmond upon Thames College. Formerly Principal of Shene Sixth Form College.

F. Janes
Principal of Yeovil College. Formerly Principal of Havering Technical College.

B. L. Pearce
Librarian at Richmond upon Thames College. Formerly Tutor Librarian at Twickenham College of Technology.

PREFACE

In this collection of essays the contributors have addressed themselves to the overriding educational problem of the 1980s, the provision to be made for the 16 to 19 age group. They argue that a national policy is long overdue and strongly recommend the tertiary college as the model of the future. In their view it combines the best traditions of the sixth form with that of the college of further education, and by virtue of its comprehensiveness may allow the development of a thorough-going post-compulsory education system in Britain.

All the contributors work at tertiary colleges but they wish to make it clear that the views they express are entirely their own and do not necessarily represent those of their colleges or Local Education Authorities.

Richmond upon Thames
1980

A. B. Cotterell
E. W. Heley

1

A HISTORY OF THE TERTIARY COLLEGE

F. Janes

Rival Systems for the 11 to 19 Group

The years since the Education Act of 1944 have seen a remarkable growth in the numbers of young people continuing their education full- or part-time after the compulsory stage, together with a growth in the number, size and variety of institutions catering for them. There is still a parallel provision under secondary and further education regulations, a divide whose origin lies in historical accident and which assumes that the customers can indeed be so precisely classified. Yet, at the raising of the school leaving age in 1973, large numbers of 15 year-olds were reclassified as 'secondary' from 'further', a move which must cast doubt on the validity of the thesis that a bipartite provision in the post-compulsory stage does reflect a natural division of young people. The thesis of this book is that the bipartite classification is invalid; that youngsters are not 'secondary' or 'further'; that each is an individual and should therefore be provided for as an individual and not as a type.

The argument here is that in students in the post-compulsory stage of education there is a natural spectrum of ability, attainment, interests and career aspirations which should determine that the age group be provided for as a whole under one set of regulations and by one all-embracing institution designed to meet the needs of each individual in that continuum. We urge the introduction of a new stage of tertiary education in our national pattern to follow the end of compulsory education at 16, a stage which is neither 'secondary' nor 'further' as they are currently known and practised but a merger of their approaches and provisions. We urge that the stage is best provided for by a single institution, the *tertiary college,* though it is recognised that in many areas the geographical distribution of educational plant dictates an initial pattern of existing institutions collaborating, under single management, to provide a coordinated service.

Tertiary education may be defined as that stage of post-compulsory education outside the higher education sector which provides the full- and part-time education of students aged 16 and over. Training is seen as part of this educative process. A tertiary college is an institution, currently administered under further education regulations but which would more appropriately be administered under a new set of tertiary regulations, designed as the sole provider in its area of full- and part-time education for students aged 16 and over. It is open-ended in that it overlaps with the higher education sector in offering some advanced courses of sub-degree level, usually part-time, where local demand justifies the provision; for example, the higher certificates of the Business and Technician Education Councils. Adult or continuing education is part of its brief.

A summary of the various education systems is shown in Fig. 1.1. We shall now examine the origins of system (e).

The Origins of Tertiary Education

The unquestioning acceptance by most educational thinkers of the divide between secondary and further education has naturally led those approaching from the secondary standpoint to concentrate upon the sixth form rather than on the 16 to 19 age group as a whole. Is GCE A-level a satisfactory form of education for today's sixth-formers? What should be the curriculum for the 'new sixth'? Above all, is the small sixth form able to provide an adequate range of education opportunity, and is it an acceptable user of scarce and expensive resources? The current anxiety over falling rolls in the 16 to 19 age group is bringing the latter question very much to the fore as we enter the 1980s.

> Even if the large cost were justified, in present times of shortage small and medium sized schools cannot fairly claim either the highly skilled staff or the equipment to make efficient tuition of each of these tiny groups (often consisting of only one or two pupils) possible... It is no accident that the plums of open scholarships regularly fall to the big schools which can organise higher education more efficiently, and can provide full-time specialist teachers virtually for Sixth Form work alone.[1]

That is not a quotation from a report by a present-day Chief Education Officer to his Education Committee; it was written 36 years ago by Robin Pedley, now Professor of Education at Southampton University. To paraphrase—the mills of education grind exceeding slow.

He was not alone in his view but it was a decade before the first, unsuccessful, proposal was made to combine small sixth forms into a sixth form college at Croydon in 1954 and yet another decade before the pioneer sixth form colleges were established at Mexborough (1964) and at Luton (1966). Today they number over one hundred, and few who know their record of achievement would challenge the view that they offer their students a markedly improved range of educational opportunity with a more effective use of resources than is possible in small sixth forms. But their existence rests upon the assumption that it is both possible and desirable to distinguish at 16 between the student who requires continued general or academic education under secondary regulations and the student who requires vocational education under further education regulations. The sixth form colleges are themselves questioning the validity of this thesis by developing their own range of 'secondary vocational' courses as alternatives to 'further education vocational' courses. There may well be justification for a variety of provision, but that in itself does not justify the existence of parallel institutions to house them. The colleges of further education have equally challenged the validity of the concept by developing the provision of 'further education academic and general' courses. Has Mother Nature been so thoughtful as to have provided two distinct types of 16 year-olds, those who require 'secondary academic, vocational and general' courses in a secondary establishment and those who require

(a) Selective Secondary System

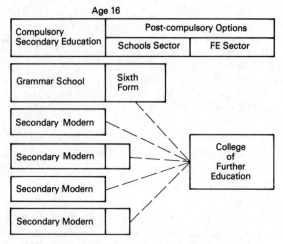

Note: *Under the selective system, some secondary modern*
schools may develop their own small sixth forms.

(b) All-through Comprehensive System

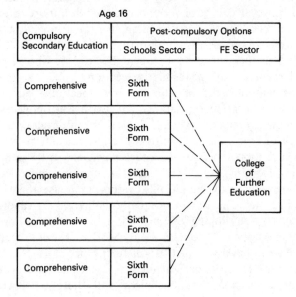

(c) Sixth Form Centre

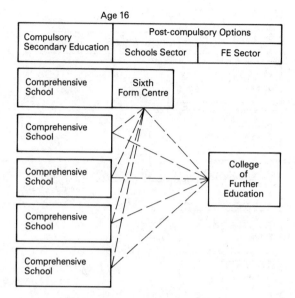

(d) Sixth Form College

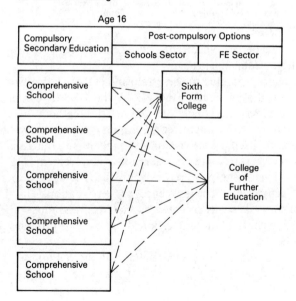

(e) Tertiary College

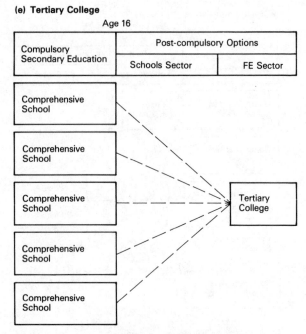

Fig. 1.1 Systems of education for 11 to 19 year-olds (Reproduced from *The Sixth Form and its Alternatives,* **1979), by kind permission of the NFER, Slough.**

'further academic, vocational and general' courses in a further education establishment?

The major stimulus to the establishment of sixth form colleges came with the publication in 1965 by the DES of *Circular 10/65* which included the concept as one of the methods by which an education authority might reorganise on comprehensive lines. But the circular itself conceived of comprehensive education only in secondary terms; the considerable involvement of further education with those over the school leaving age of 15 received scant recognition. The existence of 'two nations' in the post-compulsory stage was accepted by the DES, and most others, as a fact which should not be questioned, or, at least not questioned at that time.

However, some voices were challenging the validity of a bipartite approach in the post-compulsory stage. Nine years earlier Robin Pedley had written:

. . . there is another point of weakness in our present system . . . the gap in the education of the older adolescent during the three or four years after compulsory schooling ends. It is bridged for a favoured minority by the sixth forms of grammar schools; but . . . Nowhere is there the broad modern structure which could take the potential traffic . . .[2]

The 'broad modern structure' which Pedley had in mind was a revised version of the county college, proposed in the 1944 Education Act but which did not materialise:

. . . the real needs at this stage could only be met by a separate institution—the county college for full-time as well as part-time education between 15 and 19.[3]

Pedley made three further points:

We need a policy which first accepts in principle the rightness of providing for this age group as a whole while having regard for the great variety of opportunity needed by the individuals within it . . .[4]

The real lasting defect of the present (tripartite) system—and the introduction of comprehensive secondary schools will do nothing at all to remove it—is the retention in school (essentially a children's place) of people who are physically and to some extent intellectually mature. It ignores, too, the widening gulf which separates young workers from those who continue full-time schooling in the years of adolescence —perhaps the most vital years of all for the formation of social attitudes.[5]

We do not want to re-create Disraeli's 'two nations' in a new guise . . . both student and worker have much to learn from the other.[6]

Prophetically, he added:

All this, however, represents an ultimate aim . . . it cannot be achieved all at once.[7]

Advocacy for Institutional Change

In the 1960s the argument for a separate stage of post-compulsory education and a separate tertiary institution was taken up more widely, with two advocates being prominent: Deryck Mumford, then Principal of the Cambridgeshire College of Arts and Technology, and Sir William (now Lord) Alexander, then Secretary of the Association of Education Committees. In 1970 Mumford summarised the advantages for the 16 to 19 age group of what he called a Junior College as follows:

(1) All students who wish to continue their education beyond 16

would do so in the same institution. Junior Colleges, therefore, satisfy the principles of comprehensive education in a way no other system does.

(2) The Junior College could provide in the most economic way possible a wide range of courses to cater for all ranges of ability and for the development of specific talents. It also allows, in a way no other system does, for ease of transfer between courses for students who, for one reason or another, make the wrong choice at the beginning.

(3) With all students above the compulsory school leaving age, and attending voluntarily, it can provide the freer, more adult atmosphere appropriate to, and demanded by, young people of these age groups. With part-time students already at work and with staff experienced in the worlds of industry and commerce it would, unlike the academic sixth form college, be outward looking to the world of work and also open-ended to higher and adult education.

(4) The mixture of academic and vocational work and of full-time and part-time courses would ensure a wide range of experience, qualifications and interests among staff and students. This variety has, in itself, great educational value and provides the best conditions for the wide range of extra-curricular activities and a vigorous corporate life.

(5) It would probably be easier to staff than any other system. The wide range of work would often justify the employment of specialists who could not be fully utilised in any other system. The absence of lower level work would make posts in the Junior College more attractive than in all-through comprehensive schools to well qualified graduates with specialist interests.

(6) It is more cost effective than any other system. Numbers can often be large enough to ensure that staff are used economically and waste arising from duplication of provision for the 16 to 19 age group in schools and further education is eliminated. Because the number of Junior Colleges would be smaller than the number of sixth forms in the all-through comprehensive system the provision in all colleges of good laboratories, workshops, studios, libraries and communal facilities would be economically justified.[8]

Mumford also made a prophetically pertinent comment on the relative cost effectiveness of the tertiary college solution compared with the all-through 11 to 18 comprehensive schools. It was estimated that the latter needed between 1000 and 1500 pupils to ensure a viable sixth form. Since some 75 per cent of existing buildings at that time housed less than 600 pupils the adoption of the 11 to 18 school would require a most costly building programme; the two-tier solution of 11 to 16 comprehensive schools leading to a tertiary college would approximate more closely to the existing plant and would therefore be less expensive. In the event, a considerable number of authorities embarked on new buildings for 11 to 18 schools designed to accommodate up to 2000 pupils, an exercise which at today's prices has cost the nation several thousand million pounds. Many of these authorities are now facing the problem of sixth form numbers in those schools falling below the 70 to 100 currently regarded as viable.[9]

Lord Alexander was the first to use the term *tertiary college*. He argued that the growth of full- and part-time education since 1944 warranted a new stage in our provision, a stage of tertiary education which would replace the overlap between secondary and further education!

> It can be argued with some force that since the principle of a comprehensive approach to education is of such major concern, it should be maintained up to the age of 18... The suggestion which I now make, therefore, is that the secondary stage of education should be limited to the age of 16... and that there should be established tertiary colleges providing both full- and part-time education from this stage to 18 plus.[10]

It was only in seeing a sharp break at 18 + between tertiary colleges and higher education that Alexander differed substantially from Mumford's case. Mumford countered Alexander's view as follows:

> Many part-time technician courses planned as a unified progression would, on this system (Alexander's break at 18) be divided between tertiary and higher education colleges. When higher education has developed to such an extent that most of the population live within travelling distance of an institution of higher education such separation may become feasible. However, for many years to come, higher education courses, particularly if part-time, will have to be provided in association with non-advanced courses... it would be economically impossible in most areas at present to separate tertiary and higher education institutionally.[11]

The Establishment of Tertiary Colleges

Although the case for a new tertiary stage of education was not accepted, the argument for tertiary colleges met a few receptive ears. The first such college was established at Exeter in 1970 and others have followed:

1972   North Devon College, Barnstaple
       Nelson and Colne College
1973   Bridgwater College
       Strode College, Street
1974   Cricklade College, Andover
       S.E. Derbyshire College
       W.R. Tuson College, Preston
       Yeovil College
1975   Accrington and Rossendale College
       Crosskeys College, Gwent
1976   Leigh Tertiary College
1977   Richmond upon Thames College
1979   Oswestry College

The Abraham Moss Centre (1973), Frome College (1974) and Wigan College of Technology (1977) have strong tertiary characteristics but they do not fall clearly within the definition given earlier in this chapter. Proposals for further colleges are with the Secretary of State. In the event these colleges followed the Mumford pattern rather than that proposed by Lord Alexander. The majority were based upon an existing college of further education and have replaced the grammar/modern school structure although there are already instances where sixth form colleges or comprehensive sixth forms have been merged with further education.

The reasons given by Local Education Authorities for establishing these colleges appear to be based in differing proportions upon an ideological acceptance of the case and a realistic acceptance that the secondary-tertiary solution would most effectively and economically fit local conditions. The establishment of Yeovil College illustrates the process. The Chief Education Officer of Somerset, Bob Parker, himself convinced of the validity of the case, prepared a closely reasoned report which led to the conclusion that in towns such as Yeovil, Bridgwater and Street, where small-to-medium-sized technical colleges existed, the most educationally effective pattern of reorganisation would be 11 to 16 comprehensive secondary schools leading to tertiary colleges based upon the premises of the technical colleges. He saw the main advantages of the tertiary colleges as:

> (i) a wider range of courses offering greater flexibility of choice in the number and type of subjects taken.

(ii) the chance to break down the barriers which have tended to exist between academic and applied studies.

(iii) the chance for young people to work in a more adult atmosphere and within a social framework which will be developed in the light of present day experience and be unrestricted by any traditional attitudes.

(iv) the concentration of skilled teaching staff and expensive equipment.[12]

On his retirement in 1974, he wrote:

We have had, for most of the time since the war, a divisive system of education separating future managers and technologists from those with whom they have had to work...[13]

Hence his proposal was considered in Yeovil alongside the other structures in *Circular 10/65*. Wide local discussion led to a substantial majority of parents, teachers, managers and governors favouring the secondary – tertiary proposal. It was ultimately accepted by the County Council in 1970 and approved by the Secretary of State, Mrs Margaret Thatcher, in 1971.

Tertiary Innovations

In the English tradition each tertiary college has interpreted its brief in its own way in response to local conditions, but there is a common pattern of innovation and readiness to adapt which may be illustrated by an outline account of the establishment and development of Yeovil College.

From the outset it was accepted that the tertiary college was a new type of institution significantly different from a technical college and that the latter had effectively disappeared with the grammar and modern schools. An early decision of major significance was to replace the conventional further education departmental structure by a matrix.[14] The departmental structure, despite its undoubted administrative convenience, is the subject of increasing criticism in further education because it tends to restrict a student's programme of study to the resources available in a department rather than to those available in the college as a whole. It encourages both staff and students to see their loyalty as being due to 'their' department rather than to the college, and this inhibits the development of a corporate college life. The matrix structure adopted by Yeovil arranges the staff in 15 teaching teams, known as *schools,* whose role is to service the whole college in the teaching of its subject or subjects and to have regard for the quality of the teaching. Some schools are single-subject, for instance, English; others are a group of related disciplines such as Business and Management Studies. Students, whether full- or part-time, are the responsibility of five senior staff known as *deans of study,* who with the aid of tutors exercise pastoral care and who commission from the schools the teaching of courses and classes in the dean's own field, for example, Technology. These courses and classes are then part of the college's provision and are available to all students. The deans are the highest paid staff, after the principal and the vice-principals; the college has 'put its money where its mouth is' in placing high priority upon pastoral care. The intention of the matrix is to foster a college-based approach by staff and students, and to place emphasis upon the twin objectives of care of student and quality of teaching. It is noteworthy that most of the tertiary colleges so far established have either abandoned the departmental structure or have significantly modified it.[15]

A second major change stemmed from the first; the absence of departments necessitated a college timetable based, for full-timers, on a 'sixth form' modular approach. The full-time student under the guidance of a Dean composes his (or her) own programme of studies by selecting a balanced number of modules of examination and 'minority' studies which reflects his level of ability and attainment, his interests and career aspirations. This contrasts with the typical further education approach which tends to fit the student into one of a number of 'prepackaged' courses; Yeovil's approach is *à la carte,* not *table d'hôte*; the suit is tailor-made, not ready-made and abandons the artificial distinction between 'vocational' and 'academic' students and studies. The opportunities for developing this approach for day-release and 'training' students are restricted by the tight control over the curriculum exercised by examining bodies and the industrial training boards, but progress has been made in 'setting' English and Mathematics.

The college adopted the further education practice of encouraging an adult ethos for its students, and as anticipated this has led to mature and responsible behaviour together with a marked degree of motivation and participation. A relaxed and friendly relationship exists between staff and students very much akin to that of a university and disciplinary problems are rare. There is, nevertheless, a firm insistence that the purpose of a student's attendance at the college is to study and that continued attendance depends upon adherence to that premise. Care was taken in the appointment of the teaching staff to ensure that at all levels there was a mixture of those with secondary and those with further education experience, a factor essential if one wishes to encourage a merger of the best practices to produce a new approach. The combination provides the ingredients for a fresh look at the 16 to 19 issues which have previously largely been viewed from one angle only. The 'setting' of English for first-year day-release apprentices with specially designed teaching materials is one example of a change in approach mainly brought about by staff whose previous experience was predominantly secondary. The presence of staff with experience in the world of industry and commerce, together with the appropriate facilities of workshops and equipment, and the close links with industry and commerce provide a new dimension of resources available to those who in other patterns of 16 + provision would be sixth-formers: A-level GCE science students, for example, can and do call upon these resources in the project and research work which has been developed alongside their formal examination studies.

Each of the first generation of tertiary colleges is producing changed attitudes and approaches as it explores and develops the potential afforded by the combination of secondary and further in the single institution:

> ... a tertiary college developed from an existing college of further education... would develop fresh characteristics, modify its internal organisation (the departmental structure is not sacred), exploit the advantages conferred by size and resources, and in due course evolve into a new educational organism.[16]

Academic Consequences of Tertiary Education

What results have the new colleges achieved? Perhaps Yeovil College may be used to illustrate the pattern that is emerging from the colleges. One of the major doubts concerned their ability to maintain the academic standards associated with the traditional grammar schools. A detailed analysis of Yeovil's A-level results for

1974–78 has been published[17] and it indicates that, for comparable students, the college has maintained those standards; with those who may be regarded to as 'further education students' there has been a significant improvement. The 1979 results were very encouraging as the following summary shows:

Pass Rate	Local Grammar Schools	1972–74	79%
	Comparable students	1975–78	79%
	Comparable students	1979	83%
	Technical College	1972–74	50%
	Comparable students	1975–78	62%
	Comparable students	1979	75%

The results of the 'Annual Oxbridge Stakes', a commonly accepted measure of the standard of the most academically able, also show an improvement. Former staff of the grammar schools state that, together, the two schools usually obtained one or two places a year including an occasional Open Award; students of the former technical college did not run. The record since reorganisation is:

	Open Awards	Places
1975	1	1
1976	–	4
1977	–	2
1978	2	3
1979	3	8
1980	3	5

A team of college students won the 1977 BBC TV Young Scientists of the Year competition with a piece of industrial research and went on to be placed second in the Philips European competition. Several science students have had the results of their research published in learned journals.

A second fear is that the colleges will concentrate on full-time students at the expense of the standards of day-release students. Awards gained in the summer 1978 examinations were a City and Guilds Bronze Medal in Vehicle Body Work, a prize from the Institute of Mechanical Engineers for a girl candidate in the Higher National Certificate in Engineering examinations, and an RSA

Bronze medal for a secretarial student. In 1979 Yeovil won the National Vehicle Trades Apprentice Competition and a part-time student won a City and Guilds Medal in Engineering. A third doubt concerns the provision of a lively cultural, sporting and social life. Some 28 sports are actively pursued at Yeovil. In the first national finals of the British Association for Sport in Colleges held in 1979 Yeovil won the right to represent South Wales and the West of England in five of the twelve sports offered. In 1979 a student gained two Under-19 England cricket caps and another was capped in each of the Under-19 England Rugby matches. In December 1979 some 70 full-time and part-time students booked the Collegiate Theatre, London, for a week to stage a modern musical, Starman, with words and music written by two members of staff in collaboration with a third—from the Nelson and Colne College (another tertiary). A student toured the USA at Easter 1979 with the National Youth Theatre. Another was the soloist with the South Somerset Orchestra in a performance of a Rachmaninov Piano Concerto. The college Christian Fellowship has nearly raised the £5000 needed to convert the cellar of an old house on the campus into a crypt chapel. Perhaps it is pertinent to ask if students in the small sixth forms enjoy a similar range of opportunities.

Prospects

The 1970s have seen an increased awareness in educational and political circles that all is not well with the provision of education and training for the 16 to 19 year-old. Numerous bodies have conducted research into the needs of and provision for the age group ranging from the Schools Council Sixth Form Survey (1970) to The Sixth Form and Its Alternatives published by the National Foundation for Educational Research in 1979. In curriculum development the Schools Council has endeavoured to find agreement on what, if anything, should be done to alter GCE A-level, to provide a common examination at 16, and to develop the Certificate of Extended Education for the 'new sixth'. In the separate world of further education the Technician and Business Education Councils, established to develop a unified national system for the education of technicians, have set off with contrasting approaches, the one essentially modular and the other essentially integrated. Rising youth employment brought the Manpower Services Commission on the scene with new provision for the less able.

In institutional terms there has been an impressive growth in the number of sixth form colleges and the establishment of the first tertiary colleges. Each has given rise to the formation of new professional bodies, the Association of Principals of Sixth Form Colleges and the Tertiary College Panel. Attitudes have eased during the 1970s. An indication is given by the formation in 1975 of the Standing Conference of Sixth Form and Tertiary College Principals whose members meet in a spirit of cooperative enquiry into the education of the 16 to 19 group rather than in partisan attitudes of competition. 1979 saw the first moves by the teaching staffs in those colleges to provide a similar forum for discussion; a Northern Association was formed and exploratory meetings were held in the east and the south of the country. These associations are providing a valuable bridge leading to better understanding between secondary and further education.

As we enter the 1980s there is, to borrow a phrase, a wind of change blowing across the post-compulsory field of education. Falling rolls and rising costs are causing a serious questioning of the educational and economic viability of the small sixth form. In 1978 there were 3089 sixth forms in maintained secondary schools; that figure excludes sixth form colleges but includes the 516 sixth forms which had no A-level GCE students. Of that figure, 1507 (49 per cent) had less than 70 students and 614 (21 per cent) had less than 20.[18] There is a growing concern at the uncoordinated nature of the provision of education and training for the 16 to 19s and growing doubt as to the validity of the divide and overlap between secondary and further education. A national debate has been instituted by the Department of Education and Science with the issue in 1979 of three consultative documents: *16 – 18. The Education and Training of 16 – 18 Year Olds, Providing Educational Opportunities for the 16 – 18 Year Olds* and *A Better Start in Working Life.*

Although the number of tertiary colleges is still small and few can point to at least five years experience, the evidence so far justifies the claims made for them over the post war years by Pedley, Mumford and Alexander. The conclusions of the NFER research support the view that the interests of the 16 to 19 age group, and the interests of the nation, will best be served if the outcome of this debate is the establishment of a tertiary stage of education and the development of tertiary colleges:

> While the sixth form colleges have shown that a break at 16 can work successfully it is the tertiary colleges which point the way to a future where the two sectors are fused together and post-compulsory education is seen as a cohesive whole.[19]

Notes

1 Pedley R., in *Times Educational Supplement,* 9 Sep. 1944
2 Pedley R., *Comprehensive Education: A New Approach,* (London, Gollancz, 1956), p.61
3 *ibid.,* p.161
4 *ibid.,* p.165
5 *ibid.,* p.164
6 *ibid.,* p.165
7 *ibid.,* p.169
8 Mumford, D., *Comprehensive Reorganisation and the Junior College* (Sheffield Polytechnic, ACFHE, 1970), pp.20 – 1
9 *Providing Educational Opportunities for 16 – 18 Year Olds* (London DES, Apr. 1979), p.8
10 Alexander, W. *Towards a New Education Act* (London, Councils and Education Press Ltd., 1969), p.19
11 Mumford, D., *op.cit.,* p.14
12 Parker, R., *A Memorandum on Secondary Re-organisation: Junior Colleges* (Taunton, Somerset County Council, 1970) (unpublished)
13 Parker, R., *Somerset Education Newsletter,* Spring 1974 (unpublished)
14 *Aims and Organisation,* Yeovil College, 1975 (unpublished)
15 *Tertiary Colleges 1978,* Tertiary Colleges Panel (unpublished)
16 *After 16* (London, ACFHE/APC, 1975), p.25
17 *Head Teachers Review* (London, National Association of Head Teachers, April 1979)
18 As note 9
19 Dean, J., Bradley, K., Choppin, B. and Vincent, D., *The Sixth Form and its Alternatives* (Slough, NFER, 1979), p. 326

2

PHILOSOPHY: BEYOND EXPEDIENCY

E. W. Heley

Why do we need a philosophy?

It is the habit of the English (we cannot speak for the Celtic inhabitants of these islands) to distrust a philosophical approach to problems. At its best this attitude encourages improvisation and flexibility and has often served us well. Its disadvantage in times of rapid change is that the nation stumbles from one expedient to another. Piecemeal solutions become impediments to fundamental reform. Within a short period of time the wheel of fashion turns and we are left with incompatible structures. An obvious example of this—one that affects education—is the entirely differing criteria for size and function of the London Government Act of 1963 and the local government reform of ten years later. In the first the integrated service of Middlesex County Council was broken up and its educational responsibilities handed to the outer London boroughs. The estimable Inner London education service was only saved from a similar fate at the eleventh hour. In the second reform great cities such as Sheffield, Bristol and Southampton were declared (partly on grounds of size) to be incompetent to run services which were apparently quite safe in the hands of London suburban authorities (as indeed they are).

The hoary old tale of the French Minister of Education taking

"Like the Cheshire Cat, each major report appears and disappears at whim."

**Fig. 2.1 The trouble with piecemeal solutions.
(Reproduced by kind permission of *Times Educational Supplement.*)**

out his watch and remarking that a certain grade of pupil would throughout France be working on page 47 of the prescribed historical text—there are many versions—was told in the smug belief that such centralisation was an example of Gallic inflexibility and that things were ordered better on this side of the channel. The mobile family of today faced with innumerable and incompatible systems of education and syllabuses which arbitrarily change at county boundaries might be forgiven for wishing that our Secretary of State had such powers. We would not agree with such a potentially totalitarian formula, but clearly the present chaotic state of secondary provision and its duplication, post-16, by the further education sector is costly, confusing to parent and pupil, divisive and cannot be said to be serving the needs of the nation.

Anyone who has travelled on the continent regularly since the Second World War will be aware of the relative decline of Great Britain. The inner cities of the Federal Republic of Germany seldom exhibit the shabby decay which is so evident in ours. The price levels, so high by our standards, are met by well-paid workers who clearly enjoy a standard of living which in Britain is still reserved for the better-off members of the salaried middle class. Nor has this been a case of private affluence amid public squalor. The welfare services of our near-neighbours now surpass our own. Our public services—once so highly regarded—have fallen away. Much of our social plant is old and not being renewed. Unlike that of Paris, London's underground system, for example, is becoming dirty and on some lines dangerous. The black plastic rubbish bag on the pavement is becoming a symbol of our decline. The erosion of our industrial base and our tendency born of an imperial past, to import first and pay later have made raising the standard of our public services increasingly difficult. Indeed the need to cut public expenditure in order to reverse industrial decline is now the approved wisdom. The reasons for this lamentable change in our fortune since the war have been earnestly debated, and it would be wearisome and outside the scope of this book to rehearse them here. We would, however, wish to make a case for the proposition that the defects of our education system itself may have been a contributory factor and that any long-term prospects for improvement will depend on a thorough review of the education and training of the young. From this it must not be imagined that we are about to attack the comprehensive school in the manner of the *Black Paper* fraternity. It is self-evident that since the first comprehensive schools were created in the mid-1950s and their greatest development was in the early 1970s, no one charged with management of enterprises, institutions or our governance is likely to have been educated 'comprehensively'. If our affairs have been badly handled, the products of our private sector and unreorganised maintained schools must shoulder the blame.

Our contention is that myopia has afflicted our view of education at the point where it ceases to be a compulsory activity. We have comprehensive primary schools and comprehensive secondary schools up to the statutory leaving age, but beyond this we have confusing and unplanned provision which has grown up haphazardly and which caters still for a minority of young people. At 16 our children are divided as rigidly as they ever were at 11 in the abandoned selective school system. The big divide is between those who stay on in full-time education and those who leave school and go either into employment or to the enforced leisure of the unemployment register. Of the total population aged 16 to 18 only 30 per cent were in the first category in 1976–77. The remaining 70 per cent have a very low expectation of further education. Only 13.5 per cent of the age group are allowed day or block release.[1] Allowing generously for an unquantifiable number of young people educating themselves through evening classes, the figure for continuative education post-16 must be lower than 50 per cent, a statistic which places us educationally, if not geographically, in Mediterranean Europe.

The proportion of young people being educated by the further education sector comes as a surprise to those whose interests lie entirely in traditional sixth form work. When day-release, block release and sandwich students are taken into account the figures are: schools 18 per cent, further education 23 per cent. The further education sector has about one third of those in full-time education. In case it may be thought that the students have divided themselves neatly into 'academics' at school and 'vocationals' at college, it is interesting to note that of the 412 000 GCE/CSE students aged 16-18 in 1976–77 no fewer than 60 000 (approximately 15 per cent) were in the colleges. Naturally the overwhelming proportion of school sixth-formers are shown as engaged on GCE or CSE work. This statistic should be viewed with caution. 65 000 (or 18 per cent of school sixth-formers) are on GCE O-level/CSE programmes only. A Gresham's Law is operating in those parts of the country where employment prospects are low. Pupils with good GCE/CSE results leave school at 16 to take jobs formerly the preserve of less-able young people. Those without the prized certificates return to school as preferable to unemployment in the hope of gaining over one or two years sufficient passes to join the ranks of the employed. In this way a group euphemistically described as 'the new sixth' has developed which bears little relationship to the sixth form of hallowed memory. In more favoured areas a similar development is taking place: those

that led in voluntary staying-on when 15 was the school leaving age
are on the way to a voluntary leaving age of 17. The pass rates of
'new sixth' students in both cases is sufficiently low to cause
considerable anxiety and many head teachers use the GCE/CSE, the
only prestigious examinations available to them, in packages with a
vocational flavour.

The argument is not that young people below the acceptable sixth
form entry requirement (say four GCE O-level passes, grades A-C)
should be turned away but that there is little justification for having
some 'new sixth' pupils in schools and others often noticeably more
successful ones, in vocational courses at a local college of further
education. There were no fewer than 121000 such students in
1976–77, almost twice as many as stayed on in their schools for GCE
O-level programmes. Moreover, this figure does not include 30000
on GCE O-level programmes in colleges for whom the same critical
comments apply.

The problems of course choice and curriculum planning is dealt
with in Essay 4. Here it is sufficient to note the extraordinary
muddled state of our 16 to 19 provision.[2] Since it is seldom explained
to parents, choice, a justification for diversity, is more apparent
than real. There are only a few areas where parents and students
at 16+ are given unbiased information by the Local Education
Authority on opportunities, post-16. Areas such as
Castlepoint-Rochford in south-east Essex may be said to have a
tertiary system; 11 to 16 schools followed by an informed choice, but
these are but candles in a naughty world. Almost everywhere the
college of further education complains of lack of cooperation from
the schools and its difficulty in meeting prospective students, while
the schools complain of the 'hard sell' tactics of the local college with
its glossy brochures and shameless use of advertising techniques,
which are thought to be more appropriate to selling detergents.

Such competition, far from being healthy, is symptomatic of a
system in a state of incipient crises. The downturn in the number of
16 year-old pupils in the mid-1980s will intensify the struggle for
students: a prospect which can be pleasing to no one. It seems to us
that we need to stand back from the jungle and consider the needs of
the student, the needs of society, and the needs of the economy. If we
do not do this in time—and time is short—the inexorable decline in
student numbers coupled with the economic stringency expressed in

cash limits will allow those who do not always hold the education service high in their priorities to make decisions based on what appears expedient. An opportunity will have been lost.

The Student—An Accusative Case

It is a surprising circumstance that the student for whom the whole cloud-capped towers of administration are constructed and on whose education an Amazon of books pours forth is seldom the subject of the exercise. (We are conscious of adding to the flood, but excuse ourselves with the thought that among so many one more will make little difference to the height of the tide!) Our reader may check this for himself. If he cares to he may browse along the library shelves and observe that almost every conceivable aspect of education is dealt with—its relationship with society; with future manpower planning; its devotion to or indifference to the creation of wealth; its organisational patterns, its examination systems, actual or proposed; the role of the administrator, careers service, psychologist and so on. It is easy to conclude that like the girl in Gower's *Plain Words* we can learn more about the education service than we really want to know.

In our judgment this would be to mistake quantity for quality. There is an omission. Almost the whole of this prodigious output is concentrated on what we must do, 'we' in this context being those set in authority over our schools and colleges. How we should organise, plan and control the system: a recent example of this tendency is *What must we Teach?* by Tim Devlin and Mary Warnock.[3] This book has a somewhat blinkered school-bound approach to the curriculum and we content ourselves with commenting on the revealing title. A more student-oriented approach would have given us *What must they Learn.* The authoritarian implications of the alteration would however be too close for comfort and one which the authors would surely disown.

It is on the dustier parts of the shelves that one comes across the works of pioneers who believed that education was for the student. His needs, hopes, fears, problems and ambitions not ours should be the paramount consideration. As A. S. Neill wrote in *Summerhill:*

> No one has the right to make a boy learn Latin because learning is a matter of individual choice but if in a Latin class, a boy fools all the time

the class should throw him out because he interferes with the freedom of others.[4]

Implied here in simplest terms are a number of propositions which are particularly apt to the 16 to 18 age group, though we might disagree with A. S. Neill concerning younger pupils.

First, the student should make a free choice among genuine and fully explained alternatives. If he opts for (say) Art, Sociology and Drama, this choice should be respected provided that he is made fully aware that such a course is unlikely to lead to satisfactory employment prospects. He may well shame us from such a mercenary view of education by declaring that it is his personal development which is important!

Secondly, having made a choice, he should contract with the college or school to pursue his studies diligently, with a view to qualifying at the end of the course. The notion that freedom means that 'anything goes' is one that Neill would have found tiresome. Freedom implies complete personal responsibility, which is why it is inappropriate for children and indispensable for adults.

Lastly, it is proposed that it is the student's peers who act as a disciplinary force. It is the class and not the teacher which throws out the silly fellow. Neill is far from suggesting mob rule. The class is not a star-chamber licensed by the teacher as absolute monarch to act in an arbitrary manner, but concerned individuals asserting the rights of the class as a whole to be a civilised community.

It seems to us that these propositions are the foundation of a system of education likely to appeal to the 16 to 18 age group but that our arrangements make it difficult to adopt them. The 11 to 18 school is at the present time the mode form of the comprehensive system. (For our argument the 12 to 18, 13 to 18 and 14 to 18 schools are not different in kind, though our criticisms have less force, the narrower and older the age band. We do not care for the 14 to 18 school on other grounds. It prolongs the primary stage by the introduction of a 9 to 14 school which has yet to find a curriculum, an ethos, or a goal in our examination-oriented world.) The 11 to 18 school has an age range which is clearly untenable. The 18 year-old man, who is legally adult, often has little in common with the enthusiastic boy of the first year. Yet the school has to enforce a disciplinary code which cannot be appropriate to both. The classic remedy is to enlist the support of the sixth form in policing the lower school. It is claimed that this is an education in accepting responsibility for others. There are two objections to this notion. Before we can begin to accept responsibility for others we must understand ourselves and have experience of taking responsibility for our own lives. Without this experience and self-awareness, the sixth-former is cast in the role of a monitor. His development may be arrested rather than enhanced. It is noteworthy that many sixth-formers do not wish to be prefects. They see the role for what it is—a way of fobbing them off from real power over their own lives by substituting for self-government, the guarding of the corridors, stairs and playgrounds. We may even suspect the motives and the maturity of the 17 year-old who wants to be a prefect. The second objection is from the point of view of the boys and girls in the lower school. They are denied the chance to grow to be 'good' of their own accord, since the majority of school pupils who leave at 16 are unable to experience important leading roles in the school. They are excluded from enhancing tasks concerned with sports clubs and cultural societies and the house system (if one exists) because these are the preserve of the minority who stay on in their own schools. This often-overlooked aspect of the 11 to 18 school is itself a justification for the 11 to 16 school, so often attacked as the poor relation.

Those who have accepted the argument so far that 16 to 18 year-olds need separate consideration as a group which is voluntarily exposing itself to education, reaching out towards adult status and demanding treatment appropriate to that stage of development, may feel that an adequate case has been made for the sixth form college. This increasingly common form of organisation is popular with the staffs of former grammar schools (which with one exception all sixth form colleges previously were), is regarded with confidence by parents, and is acceptable to students. We must confess that we see the sixth form college as a staging post on the highway to the tertiary college. While with one exception they are open-access or claim to be so, the menu is no more comprehensive than that of the sixth form of large 11 to 18 schools. Sixth form colleges are a reasonable solution to the needs of the 16 to 18 student in terms of social and developmental aspects of education, but they are still in competition with the college of further education for students. The choice for students is often between the resources available at the latter and the genteel poverty but prestige value of the former. The problem of the 'new sixth' is not solved. That indeed the number of such students grows rapidly in sixth form colleges is perhaps due to the feeling on the part of former secondary modern pupils that they have entered the grammar school at last. Once all 16+ provision is in institutions designed for the age group, the fatuity of two separate types of institution serving one area will be plain to see. If in seeking to avoid wasteful duplication in traditional sixth form work the college of further education is precluded from offering GCE A-levels, then the grammar school/secondary modern relationship so recently abandoned at 11 is reconstituted at 16. If on the other hand such duplication is allowed in the interest of choice, then DES surveys have shown that it is the less academically able and less well qualified A-level students who tend to opt for the college of further education. A Gilbertian situation results where those more likely to do well stay in sixth form colleges where often every resource but human ones is markedly inferior, while those less likely to be successful attend further education colleges where good libraries, common rooms, refectories, computer installations, reprographic services and ancillary help of all kinds is taken for granted.

Although damaging, this distortion is not the only example of problems engendered by the competition for students at 16. The school (and sixth form colleges are schools too) is largely ignorant of the alternative routes to the professions and technician occupations available to the able and the average pupil in the further education sector. It is regrettable, for example, that the diploma courses of the Business and Technician Education Councils are followed by only a tiny proportion of young people in full-time education, despite the fact they are accepted by professional bodies, polytechnics, industry and commerce, and *mirabile dictu* by some universities. It is tragic considering their strong orientation to our economic life. Students on these 'vocational' courses usually enjoy them and obtain good jobs or entrance to higher education when they complete the course successfully. The paucity of students is almost certainly due to lack of information, to some degree of pressure on able youngsters to remain at school, and to the low prestige attaching to the local technical college, especially in southern England.

Are we then suggesting that all post-16 education should be transferred to the college of further education? Emphatically not! A tertiary college is a comprehensive college and forms a natural third stage in areas where school provision ends at 16. It is under further education regulations because only in this way can it offer a full range of opportunity and recruit suitable staff in all areas of the curriculum (some of whom would not be recognised teachers for school work). It matters not a jot whether it is based on sixth form colleges with traditional further education added to it as in Preston, starts life as an ordinary college of further education as in Yeovil, is purpose built as in Andover, or is a merger of a college of technology and sixth form colleges as in Richmond upon Thames. What is important is that it should be genuinely open-access.

Open access is more than a statement of intent; it colours the whole enterprise. In such a college the programmes on offer have to be those the young people need. The size of the programme for the less able has to be adjusted to the numbers coming forward and not to some preordained share of resources allowed to it as against more rewarding courses in terms of Burnham points. Open access implies close liaison with schools over student placement and over curriculum. The educational programme on offer in the tertiary college should build on the foundations laid in its feeder schools. The relationship is a partnership and needs to be seen as such by all partners. Open access at a tertiary college means that the student cannot be told to go elsewhere—as he can be by both schools and further education colleges. There is no 'elsewhere'. If he is not yet qualified for the course he wants, then it is at the college he must get the necessary qualifications.

The tertiary college is a student-oriented and not a teacher-oriented institution. It seems to us that all too frequently the arguments used to defend the school sixth form are teacher-biased. Is it not said that the possession of a thriving sixth form is the hallmark of the successful secondary school and one that has stood the test of time? How typically English to invest a comparatively recent development with the patina of antiquity. Within the maintained system of education the large sixth form is probably no older than the early 1950s, when Burnham arrangements made the growth of the sixth form so advantageous in salary terms for the teachers of a school. In the 1930s and 1940s only the grammar school along with some technical schools had sixth forms. The latter were small groups of students engaged in a specialised vocational course that led to university entrance. All other forms of education and training were the province of further education and employers. When arguing that the 11 to 16 school would not be able to recruit teachers of sufficient calibre, it is overlooked that until recently the majority of our schools were for those under 15. In any case the organisation of our schools is not for the benefit of teachers but the pupils. There is no evidence that teachers do not wish to teach in all ability 11 to 16 schools provided these are of sufficient size to allow for reasonable promotion prospects. As mentioned earlier, a merit of this type of school is the opportunity it affords to all pupils to take the responsibilities and enjoy the privileges of belonging to the oldest age group. Everyone leaves the school together.[5]

Half Our Future

In 1963 John Newsom, the Director of Education of Hertfordshire, was the author of a report entitled *Half our Future*.[6] The half that the distinguished educationist had in mind was made up of those whose IQ was below 100. We have since then progressed towards the goals he set for educating the less-able half of our children. Any study of the inner city school would however dispel any tendency to complacency. The tertiary college has, of course, a splendid role to play in encouraging young people of average and below-average abilities to continue with relevant studies in a caring, democratic and non-élitist atmosphere. It is not that particular half of the population to which we would draw attention at this stage. We are referring to the half known as women!

This century has witnessed great changes in the status and opportunities for the personal fulfilment of women. Yet there is still a long way to go before women enjoy full equality with men. No great advance is made without here and there a backward step, and it is within the education system itself that changes in the organisation of schools have sometimes hindered the cause of women. It is difficult to refute the view expressed by supporters of single-sex education that the gradual disappearance of girls' schools has tended to reinforce sexual stereotyping. In girls' schools, science, mathematics and practical subjects are normal curriculum subjects and not thought, as so often in mixed schools, to be male interests. Whether the social advantages of coeducation outweigh what in any case may prove a temporary failing only time will tell. It is certainly true that for one group of women, schoolmistresses, the drift to coeducation has seen a reduction in opportunity. Yet this probably owes more to the sexism of local councillors, often elderly, than to any inherent factor in the schools themselves. The absence for a vital part of their career to raise a family also prejudices married women, a majority among women teachers.

It is now illegal to distinguish boys' subjects and girls' subjects within school or college. This ruling may in time help to break down barriers, but as in other contexts law by itself does not make us good so much as set a climate.

The college of further education with its sensitivity to its market has tended to reflect the low status of employment open to women. Until recently some further education colleges had departments of 'Women's Subjects', the implication being that the other departments were for men—as indeed they often were in terms of staffing and student enrolment. The majority of young women were engaged on secretarial courses, in catering or the 'caring' occupations, pre-nursing, nursery nursing and so forth. It was only in these fields that women held high positions in the college, but often ones subordinate to a male head of faculty. Where at one college, because of its particular history, the majority of the students were girls, the principal had to assuage the sense of shock felt by some of his visitors at so extraordinary a phenomenon. Sixth form colleges, serving very well as they do the needs of the most able, have a better balance between the sexes. However, the large number of girls in them is in part a response to the difficulties girls experience in employment and further education. The low proportion of young people at work who get day release (referred to earlier in the chapter) disguises the abysmal proportion of young women. The figure in 1978 was only 18 per cent of the total. If girls are to qualify for any worthwhile occupation, it has been decreed by the employers that it shall be through full-time education.

Our present arrangements of full-time education dictate that unless a girl is willing to entertain a restricted diet of courses leading to stereotyped subordinate roles, she must continue in full-time education along the academic road. Her brother may choose the parallel road of vocational training/further education and has a choice of full- or part-time study, sometimes with remuneration from an Industry Training Board. The merit of the tertiary college is that it puts both roads under one aegis. This does not of itself change much—a college might see itself as a bilateral institution—but it alone makes possible a change of direction. There is an opportunity to acquaint girls with the many opportunities in the technical field. In the age of the microprocessor and automation the argument for male exclusivity based on strength loses whatever validity it may have had. It would be difficult to give any reason why a well qualified woman should not be appointed to a post as a sales engineer, design engineer, draughtsman, commissioning engineer, maintenance engineer, applications engineer, cost engineer, quality engineer, jig tool designer, circuit designer, progress engineer, contract engineer, patent officer, systems engineer, work study engineer, reliability engineer, technical writer, teacher of technological subjects, purchasing engineer, contract supervisor, research and development engineer, piping designer, plant-layout engineer, manufacturing engineer, estimator or quantity surveyor. This list, which is not exhaustive, is taken from the engineering and construction careers section in a tertiary college brochure. Not many boys in our schools, let alone girls, realise that engineers are not the oily operatives of popular imagination but skilled craftsmen, technicians or professionals, in a wide variety of important and interesting jobs. In a tertiary college the 'academic' young people study alongside those on vocational courses. They cannot help but be influenced by the presence of such diversity and even the least observant among them may notice the workshops and wonder what goes on in them.

In the business and administration field it is heartbreaking to see so many girls opting for the spurious glamour of secretarial training with the aim of becoming a personal assistant and spurning the courses of the Business Education Council: courses leading to well remunerated posts with promotion prospects as an individual instead of a secretary's status which is dependent on that of her boss! Are we to believe that women are not capable of being accountants, actuaries, systems analysts, insurance adjusters, book-keepers, programmers and so on? Schools must be dissuaded from labelling typing classes as 'Commerce' and giving business education opportunities to the less able only. Programming girls for low-level jobs begins early. The comics and magazine literature so many girls read reinforce the view that girls should not aim too high and that the greatest achievement for a girl is winning a 'fella'. In *Catching Them Young* Bob Dixon shows how a typical strip romantic story makes the point that books are for squares, students, never for girls.[7]

Society cannot afford to waste the talents of women. The tertiary college may be the anvil on which a more sensible non-sexist education may be hammered out.

The Comprehensive College

In this chapter a number of inter-related themes have been explored. It has been argued that the dismal economic performance of the country may be caused in part by the failures of our education system to keep pace with our needs. We have noted how the comprehensive school for the pupil of statutory school age leads us to the concept of the comprehensive college for the 16 to 19 age group, and that since the education at that stage is voluntary the college will be a student centred institution. We have noted the abysmal record of part-time opportunities for the young worker, quite confounding the optimism of the early 1960s, when in *Day Release* (the Henniker-Heaton report) it was confidently expected that the numbers would grow and that by 1970 there would be 250 000 additional day-release students as compared with 1964.[8] Day release had by 1980 shown a slight fall on even the 1964 figure.

The tertiary institution, with its high academic standards, commitment to vocational education, and integration with the community it serves, can have a special role in part-time education. This role can extend to education as a life-long enterprise—mother, father, sixth-former and young worker using the college and its resources as unselfconsciously as they do any other public service.

The school leaving age is rising in all the countries of the developed world. The reasons for this are diverse. Rich societies can afford for all their children what rich individuals have always purchased for theirs; the growing structural unemployment of the young under the impact of new technology; the greater complexity of life and the inadequacy of the simple skills once thought sufficient for the majority of the population; the desire for learning where this has not been suppressed by authoritarian and inappropriate schooling; the coming of age of the comprehensive ideal which at its best promotes the idea of learning and culture as being the birthright of every boy and girl rather than a prize offered to those who happen to have affluent parents, or who as a compensation for neglecting such an advantage were endowed with superior mental equipment by the Almighty.

It will be inconceivable when all 16 to 18 year-olds receive full- or part-time education as of right—the next great educational advance—that they will either be able or happy to remain in schools. Schools are for children, a protected environment, essential for their secure upbringing. We maintain that the 16 to 18 year-old is a young adult requiring a stimulating free community institution in which to grow and mature.

Notes

1   *Report Number 94* (London, DES, Dec. 1978), pp. 2 – 3
2   The muddle is made even more confusing by the activities of the Industry Training Boards and the Manpower Services Commission which operate outside the education system and the purview of the DES —a peculiar anomaly
3   Devlin, T. and Warnock, W., *What Must We Teach?* (London, Temple-Smith 1977)
4   Neill, A. S., *Summerhill* (London, Gollancz, 1962), p. 309
5   Everyone would leave together if we required a full five years secondary schooling and abolished Easter leaving
6   *Half our Future:* Report of the Central Advisory Council, Newsom Report (London, HMSO, 1963)
7   Dixon, B., *Catching Them Young* (London, Pluto Press, 1977), vol. 2: *Political Ideas in Children's Fiction,* pp. 33 – 4
8   *Day Release:* Report of the Committee of Inquiry under the Chairmanship of C. Henniker-Heaton (London, HMSO, 1964) chap. 5

3

ORGANISATION AND CLIMATE: IDEALS AND ACTUALITIES

J. W. Ballard

Appropriate organisation, like appropriate technology, must match need. In the case of a tertiary college the need is that of satisfying the expectations and requirements of:

the Local Education Authority, and by implication the Department of Education and Science
the officers of the Council
ratepayers through the Council
parents
pressure groups, such as the Association for the Advancement of State Education
the governing body, and other advisory bodies which include industrial representatives and reflect regional commitments to industrial sponsors
teaching staff
principal
students

in respect of the LEA's provision for its 16+ academic and vocational education (full- and part-time) under one organisational roof.

Modern organisation theory suggests that the principles valid in hospitals, factories and offices will also be effective in colleges, and experience goes a long way toward supporting this contention.[1] To the extent that these principles involve effective participation, influence and consultation, and therefore depend on apt participatory and communication structures, the parallel holds true. Thus the arrangement of the formal groups within the college, and the college's relation to the wider environment of which it is part—both of which will have considerable influence on its activities—can be analysed and structured appropriately.

However, there are, inevitably, considerations peculiar to the individual case; considerations peculiar to education and others unique to the tertiary concept or to individual institutions. Yet experience in one tertiary college would seem very likely to echo that in others, and thus there may be value in placing something of Richmond upon Thames College's experience on record.

Organisational Expectations and Requirements

How are the different categories of people involved in the tertiary situation likely to see themselves and the college, both before and after its formation? Those outside a college will be considered first, then those inside—teachers, principal, students.

There is no doubt that Local Education Authorities facing comprehensive reorganisation schemes have been influenced by economic factors and that the importance of this aspect will become the more pronounced as numbers in the school population decline. The economic argument has not predominated in the proposals presented to the public, and pressure groups such as the Association for the Advancement of State Education, have been able to ensure that the educational factors are kept to the fore. In fact, tertiary colleges are likely to meet educational aims and, because teaching is a labour-intensive activity, economic ones as well.

Both the political left and right are likely to be concerned about bright students, and from their different standpoints to wonder whether the new institution will make the most of their potential. Articulate parents who come from grammar or private school backgrounds will compare the new institutions with their image of the old. They will remember the traditional GCE A-level sixth form and they will expect opportunities to be created for students to exercise responsibility through a 'head boy' or prefect system or through participation in activities of the 'Oxford Union' or 'Cambridge Footlights' pattern, and participation in some of the many other performing arts and extracurricular activities. Such a predilection must be kept in view but as one of many viewpoints.

No steps have been taken by the Department of Education and Science to form a 'tertiary inspectorate' or to integrate the bipartite schools and further education sectors. Because schools and further education regulations differ, it is also the case that LEA education departments incorporate a corresponding division. The tertiary college is therefore an institution which has been created in response to local circumstances and not, as in Sweden, as a result of extensive research or debate at a national level. This new type of college can only be operated under further education regulations and this fact has helped to determine its characteristics and organisation. The composition and scope of governing bodies, the scale of resources, the 'open' and adult ambience, and the nature of external and internal communication and control, all reflect this. Indeed, it is hard to see that successful tertiary institutions could have emerged within any other existing framework. There can be no question of adopting schools regulations, but there are aspects in which the articles of government and Burnham course and salary gradings inhibit the ability of the college to respond to situations as they arise.

Where a tertiary college solution has been adopted, the size of the college has not been planned but has resulted from the demands of the catchment area. The circumstance of size gives rise to one of the most well defined concerns of parents, namely that there will be some students who are not mature enough for the new environment or, for reasons of temperament, not best suited to it. 'Large' may be thought to equate with 'impersonal' and 'uncaring', and there is the real fear that individuals may get lost in the crowd. Thus any form of organisation must take full account of these concerns and the overall structure must be broken down into units with which the student can identify.

On a local basis both the management and union side of industry have interests in the range of work offered by the colleges. Representation may be via governing bodies, advisory committees, or through the sponsored students who are at the college. In the same way that parents are concerned that academic standards shall be maintained, industrialists are concerned that the applied components of vocationally oriented courses shall not be weakened. The emphasis on the dichotomy between training and education expressed by the Industry Training Boards will need to be reflected in the different organisation required for the two types of activity.

Musgrave's[2] conclusions lead one to believe that lecturers and teachers may have joined the profession because they see it as a way of keeping in touch with a favourite subject; because they have an affinity with young people; for security, and for the advantages which shorter working days and long holidays bring; or from permutations of these and other factors, leaving aside the old libel 'those who can't, teach'. In general, the desire for security has primacy over the need for achievement, and this criterion has been met to such an extent in the modern local government system that an LEA may often find itself as unable to dismiss an incompetent teacher as it is to reward the deserving. The natural wish for security can also be satisfied by membership of small working groups, and continuity ensured by the apparently never-ending supply of students to the system. Though secondary rolls are falling, this may be compensated in the tertiary structure by the continuing increase in the staying-on rate which is even now not high when compared with that of many other countries with advanced technologies. The affinity with students can be identified with a desire, conscious or not, to help young people to discover and develop themselves in what are their formative years, indicating the mutual desirability of a tutorial as well as a subject-teaching relationship.

In the light of these factors it can be seen that the setting up of a tertiary college from school and college components may well be thought to threaten the supportive and satisfying climate in a number of ways.

Although a majority of staff will welcome the challenge of change, some members of staff might feel their contribution and status both in the college and in their subject disciplines threatened. The causes for this sense of insecurity might range from anxiety that certain courses, particularly higher-level ones, would be curtailed, to the fear that, whereas each component institution has a head of subject, only one would be required in the combined situations. Conditions of service differ under further education and school regulations, and this too poses the need to adapt to a changed situation. Staff working within school regulations appreciated that they could be expected to undertake an evening commitment, and that the normal teaching day could be extended until at least 5.00 pm, while staff already under further education regulations are aware that job satisfaction and promotion prospects could be affected by a requirement to include a greater amount of school type work in their timetables.

Anxiety can be seen as normal reaction to a new situation which confronts us with unknown factors and involves unsought change. In such circumstances the group tends to draw together and to act defensively against those elements which it scents marauding on its perimeters. It is these instinctive fears which have to be soothed. Confidence has to be built up and to do so requires thought, new structures, patience and the devotion of considerable time.

Staff entering a new situation, whether from school or college, can be expected to be looking for an organisation in which there will be a recognition of their needs and status. Older members of staff, for example, are less likely to wish to take on new responsibilities, but their continuing membership of stable friendly working groups will be important to them. Participation and competition are normal dimensions to the teacher in his classroom work and the wider implications of his participation in the organisation of the college must be understood. Staff expect to observe college policy in terms of homework set, preparation of practical exercises and participation in extracurricular activities, but if these quotas are to remain high then it will be important that staff participate in formulating development plans for the college.

Research by Tannenbaum and Smith[3] suggests that in terms of staff loyalty and efficiency the degree of their actual influence relative to the principal is not so important as that they should possess channels by which they are able to or at least believe they are able to exert influence.

The principal will play an important part in creating the climate in a tertiary college. His is the central role, both in internal relationships and in the college's relationships with the local authority, parents, and other 'external groups'. His personality and style will influence much of what is said and done about the college, not only by those inside it but by those without. For this reason, as well as the need to create structures, consult with interested parties, and select his staff, he is likely to be appointed a year or so before the starting date of the college. The type of person required for the principal and the role to be filled deserves far greater consideration than is normally given. His appointment will have resulted from a favourable reaction to the exercise of charisma on a particular day before a group of people who may have had little informed idea—or not all the same idea—of the educational aims of the institution they are trying to establish. Furthermore, since tertiary colleges are such a recent development, and their size and range of work varies so much, very few principals can have had ideal experience. This is no bad thing, as they would expect to adopt the resources that they find awaiting them and to adapt their plans, to some extent, accordingly, seeing their key role as that of providing encouragement and harnessing the talent already present in the college.

Because of the complexity of skills represented in an institution of this sort, the principal will not expect to be able to exercise close control over the staff acting in their capacity as professional specialists, acknowledging that he does not share their expertise, but he will expect to have responsibility for coordinating their work. As seen by Halpin,[4] the principal will expect to act as a problem-solver or decision-maker, and as a group leader concerned with the achievement of aims and the maintenance of morale. The principal will expect to stimulate, coordinate and guide the growth of the college and the work of the staff. If they are to be aware that he is working to develop this supportive climate they must be able to see that he is approachable, receptive, and willing to listen. A daily 'surgery' and a controlled but open office door help to establish this understanding. The best of leaders will be of no use if he is not accessible, and he must be prepared to seek out problems as well as have them brought to him. Most tertiary colleges have resulted from amalgamations of separate institutions, and it has been seen that many staff may have real or imagined grievances. Quite often it is only the principal who can restore confidence.

The stress involved in the teaching profession and in dealing with the post-16 year-old is considerable. Notice must be taken by principals of articles like that by Dunham[5] which identify ways of minimising stress for heads of department through improved clerical support, staff in-service training, up-to-date job definitions and good communications. Equally the principal must make his expectations clear, for example, on student conduct and see that they are fulfilled.

The tertiary college with its associations with industry, adult education, and part-time students and staff, has 'open' boundaries, and the principal himself experiences a climate which produces pressures and demands in several important ways.

Sponsors are many and varied and include, for example, the Industry Training Boards, whose officers may affect the degree of the principal's autonomy and exert pressure in a more detailed way than the Local Education Authority or the Department of Education and Science, owing to their need to ensure that courses operate to strict industrial standards and to the fact that industry meets the cost of the courses. Parents continue to be important sponsors and to make demands at the post-16 stage, but gradually the student becomes independent of the parent and may himself become the sponsor. In the case of the industrially based part-time student the employer supersedes the parent.

The Local Education Authority controls the technical support given to the principal which includes not only the obvious material provision in terms of equipment and accommodation (for the basic teaching programme) but also such things as the number of staff, the in-service training budget and the provision of theatres, sports halls, and common rooms, around which informal teaching and social experience can revolve. One can readily identify the ambiguity and insecurity of the principal's role. When an authority needs help, the principal is regarded as one of the central administrative team; but when he has problems with the local community, or is the advocate of some aspect of the college work against external pressure, he becomes a dispensable maverick.

The majority of people in a tertiary college will be students; it is for their education that it exists and the organisation and climate must be student-oriented. The 'climate' of the college must satisfy a need for security which is in itself ambiguous—support with freedom—and for career or higher education learning opportunities in an environment affording scope for personal development. The tertiary type of college which can offer courses ranging from those for the educationally sub-normal to those for Oxbridge candidates is bound to produce some disparities in behaviour patterns which are compounded by the presence of part-time students who come from commercial and industrial backgrounds of many kinds. The climate in the college may or may not be in line with the social standards of home or peers or the technical environment of the work situation. Most colleges refer to their 'adult' atmosphere but this can have many interpretations.

In the tertiary college most full-time students are willing clients though in some cases they are subject to parental pressures. The part-time student, whose attendance is part of an employment agreement may reject or appear to reject his course, either because he himself sees little relevance between what the college has to offer and his own particular work or promotion prospects. Generally speaking, however, such reservations are few and where they exist usually related to the non-vocational component of the course, the relevance of which he and—nowadays only occasionally—his employer may not always see. Most employers place great emphasis on college achievement, and it has been pointed out that 'while low achievement and poor motivation may have their causes in personal and social problems and need immediate solutions, a good curriculum, well taught, is also an agent of care'.[6]

The tertiary college, we argue elsewhere, is well placed to organise a curriculum relevant to students' needs. Indeed the sense of confidence and achievement gained after career-oriented education is very marked. But students also expect to find within the environment of the college an opportunity for expressive faculties to develop, while the learning of social skills, inter-personal sensitivity and international understanding is facilitated through participation in student-run activities and the various sports and clubs. In fact the creation of a supportive climate is of the utmost importance. Less-able students and those with 'weak' home backgrounds need to know that someone cares about their problems. Concern should embrace both staff and students.

In all colleges there is the growing problems of a static employment situation which is increasing the gap between the age of the student and the age of the members of staff, and this will affect the climate experienced by students. This is offset in the tertiary college since many lecturers will have direct experience of the world of work and this enables them to play a particularly helpful role in the guidance process. Staff of all ages have their contribution to make, as in the human family, but young or old it is of prime importance that lecturers should view all students as equal members of a balanced community.

Musgrove[7] found that emotional security and freedom are needs of young people which are satisfied at work and at home and in social relationships but which appear to be unsatisfied at school. From their inception tertiary colleges have set out to confound the 'lack of pastoral care' criticism often levelled at technical colleges and have adopted elaborate pastoral organisations to support the learning objectives. From conversations with able students it would appear that there is a growing desire to be able to plan their own programmes tempered by an acknowledgement that they need active pressure to make them work to capacity. With the lower ability groups in the tertiary college who are sometimes not well motivated this active pressure may be achieved by programming for rather limited free time and for supervised private study. All students can be encouraged to make use of the library's facilities, however, and depending on the type, nature and level of their course, they can be given freedom to plan their programmes for homework and the use of free time. Tertiary colleges have normally followed the further education 'open campus' approach, which allows students the freedom to attend the college only during lecture periods but not the freedom to attend only selected lectures.

Intolerances sometimes found in the more rigid divided institutions between students in different departments do not appear to be so apparent in those tertiary colleges which have adopted a matrix system of organisation and where students from different divisions can meet in common teaching areas. The comprehensive nature of the tertiary college student body does mean that the future manager and future worker study, eat and play side by side, and while claims for complete social integration would be exaggerated a high degree of social tolerance is evident. School friendship groups are likely to be broken but new patterns quickly emerge within a new framework. In the secondary schools there has been a movement away from the form as a teaching unit towards participation by the pupil in a number of different 'teaching' or 'subject' groups. The patterns in the college are therefore familiar except that there may be a reversion to group identity in vocational courses of the National Diploma or Business Education Council pattern. All in all—in common with organisations in many fields of human activity—the college reflects an 'organic solidarity' as defined by Bernstein, 'where individuals relate through a complex interdependence of specialised social functions'.[8]

These, then are some of the factors to be taken into account in organisation and climate planning. Particular points which emerge include the need for students to be able to select an individual programme from a variety of vocational and academic subject areas; the avoidance of a divisive atmosphere created by too sharp a split into student divisions, emphasised for example, if there are separate divisional common rooms; the need for a structure that leads to effective course planning; the need for a pastoral organisation related to the tutorial and divisional structure; the need in timetabling to provide for student freedom in planning, for example, their own use of free time; and the need to plan for the maximum staff-student interaction.

What organisational and climate patterns will be best suited to this variety of needs and expectations, bearing in mind that appropriate organisation must match not only need but the inherited situation and the resources available?

The Tertiary Inheritance

The establishment of tertiary colleges has meant the bringing together of staff from a variety of backgrounds (grammar school, college of technology, college of further education, sixth form college and secondary modern school) in institutions which provide for students of all abilities, part-time and full-time, vocational and academic. They have been faced with the task of maintaining the traditions of high academic achievement, education for life and industrial expertise in a new and usually amalgamated institution. In the Somerset colleges and at Richmond, principal emphasis has been placed on the tertiary college as a new type of educational establishment to be developed and organised with the needs of the full-time 16 to 19 student particularly in mind.

In the social atmosphere of the 1960s students, particularly from secondary modern schools, were attracted towards colleges of further education, where ideas about independence and their desire for a greater measure of freedom could find fulfilment. This was in line with agitation for greater participation in further and higher education by students both at home and abroad, and the period was marked by a lowering of the age of majority and electoral eligibility and by the inclusion of students on college governing bodies and academic boards. Students wanted to be treated as adults, and in some cases to take advantage of a second chance to find success. Heads of schools and colleges had therefore to take note of the social pressures of the time. Staff concerned with post-16 students have had to establish new forms of relationship based upon mutual responsibility and trust. Regulations about such things as dress and smoking were modified and special common rooms or social centre facilities were introduced.

Discussions about reorganisation highlighted fundamental differences in conception between schools and colleges which have to be taken into consideration when planning for change. College departments based on assemblages of courses and led by forceful heads of department can be contrasted with the simple line management of the typical school where the Head teacher may operate as a benevolent despot. The further education college principal, on the other hand, may be seen as a monarchal intermediary between belligerent heads of department or, alternatively, as a non-accountable entrepreneur who might achieve much on behalf of his staff and students.

Neither of these leadership models are appropriate to the open-access tertiary college. It is too complex for simple line management and the centrifugal tendencies of further-education-style departments would endanger the comprehensive principles of tertiary education. In this context a possible solution is the matrix organisation.

The Matrix Organisation

Various forms of matrix organisation can be devised (see Fig. 3.1). The one illustrated in the next two figures is in use at Richmond upon Thames College and has the virtue of separating the function of curriculum planning, student enrolment, and student care from the teaching function.

The relative importance attached to non-teaching activities can be judged by the rank allotted to the leaders of the staff teams and

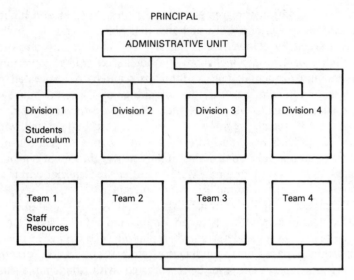

Fig. 3.1 A possible matrix organisation.

the student divisions respectively. At both Yeovil and Richmond Colleges it is the latter who are appointed to the higher Burnham grade. Both institutions claim to be student-centred, so that the relative grades of the appointments reflect a wish on the part of the respective authorities to maintain the traditions of student care claimed by the schools.

The size of the staff teams is deliberately kept small, 10 – 20, so that the control span of the team leader is effective, and the size of the student divisions to that of a reasonable sixth form, about 250. The suggested size of staff team can be housed in a larger classroom and this can be seen as a work space which will encourage the exchange of ideas and the discussion of problems.

The core of the matrix system is the idea that a member of staff shall have more than one role, more than one 'boss'. In the tertiary college the member of staff acts as a member of a team under the supervision of the team leader and also probably as a member of a group of tutors or a curriculum-coordinating group responsible to the student division head. Here it is important to consider what has happened to the administrative units which were included in each of the old further education departmental units. It is difficult when the

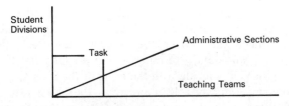

Fig. 3.2 The three-dimensional matrix.

large unit is split to justify individual administrative support. It is more convenient to consider a centralised administrative unit arranged as a number of sections along a third axis, as shown in Fig. 3.2.

We now look in more detail at the organisation pattern in use at Richmond. We begin with the 'principalship' shown in Fig. 3.3. The concept of principalship—speaking with one voice and with the authority of the principal—means that delegation with authority can take place, that the principalship group can be task-oriented. The use of the rank of assistant principal rather than associate principal gives appropriate status to the post, does not distinguish between the individuals forming the group, and does not question the ultimate authority of the principal.

The allocation of specific roles will depend upon the particular expertise and personalities of the individuals involved. Effective leadership can only occur if it is based on personal qualities rather than authority—a truth that is equally applicable to the relationship between directors and team leaders. It is also important that the assistant principals see themselves as equal contributors to the team and show a willingness to compensate for one anothers weaknesses and complement one anothers strengths. However, although flexibility is essential and the principalship is task-oriented, the task for each individual are kept within broad areas to assist liaison. Their role will vary as the workload changes

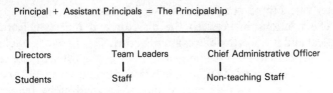

Fig. 3.3 The principalship.

or grows over a period of time and can develop to match the strengths of the individuals. At present in Richmond upon Thames College they cover the students—divisions, teaching staff—curriculum, and resources—non-teaching staff areas respectively which coincide with the arms of the matrix.

Without any doubt the role of director in the matrix structure is a most difficult one. In the short space of a year or two the director is expected to know and minister to the needs of some 250 full-time equivalent students and to have their details at his finger-tips. The process starts with interviews in the secondary schools and in the college from which data about academic potential and welfare are recorded. This in turn is transmitted to a group of 15 tutors who have no line responsibility to the director, but who must be led and developed into a front-line caring and monitoring team. Each tutor has a line responsibility to his team leader for all of his work but his tutor/teacher role does engender the feeling of working for two masters and sometimes leads to a conflict of loyalty.

All of the directors are paid on the same salary scale—as are the team leaders on theirs—a most important point in establishing equality of status for all subject areas and categories of work, whether 'academic', 'craft' or 'technological'. It also helps to ensure that advice to students is unbiased. To keep a rough balance in loads of work, groups of students can be moved from one division to another and this facility does enable new developments to be introduced or growth to be controlled.

The case for heterogeneous or homogeneous student divisions is arguable. The former are only practicable where the division and tutor group can meet regularly and establish a corporate identity distinct from any course or subject allegiance. Failing this, student divisions based on subject areas and tutor groups in which the tutor teaches the student have advantages. In the former case the director of division can be appointed solely for his personal qualities; in the latter case subject specialism is also a factor.

The relationship between the director and the team leader is critical and it is worthwhile examining this. The director establishes the curriculum and recommends a target enrolment for each subject or course to the academic board. He interviews and accepts the students. Within an agreed manpower budget he requests a teaching and administrative service from one or more team leaders.

At all stages he should consult with the team leader on subject options, size of groups, ability range of student and so on. The director's 'headmaster' talents must not only be towards the student but towards the team leaders and staff as well. He must be able to exercise command without authority. The team leader, on the other hand, has a line responsibility for his staff and he will be responsible for their performance in their teaching, tutorial and administrative roles. He will deploy them to meet the requests of the directors in what he considers to be the best possible way. Some of the qualities which directors need in their new role have been defined as tolerance of ambiguity, powers of persuasion and technical competence.

Information flow in a matrix system is necessarily large, and this is processed by the secretariats and the clerical sections under the guidance of a chief administrative officer. The entire success of the matrix college ideal can be prejudiced unless it is recognised that procedures and systems need to change to take into account differences in patterns of information flow. There will, for example, be more liaison between directors than between heads in the more traditional departmental structure and in all institutions very close cooperation is required between teaching and administrative staff to ensure that their 'paperwork' is mutually supportive. Agreement in the design of forms is essential, for example, so that both completion and processing is facilitated.

In terms of college policy, the distinction between the role of the academic board and that of the principal is an important one. From the articles of government of a college of further education it is clear that the principal is 'responsible to the governors for the internal organisation, management and discipline of the college'. In consultation with the academic board he is responsible too, for advising the governors as to the number and grading of teaching staff and the financial requirements of the college. These responsibilities are distinct from those of the academic board, which subject to the overall responsibilities of the governing body, is, 'responsible for the planning, coordination, development and oversight of the academic work of the college, including arrangements for the admission and examination of students'. A summary of the Government at Richmond is shown in Fig. 3.4.

Academic planning, its coordination and balance, will determine

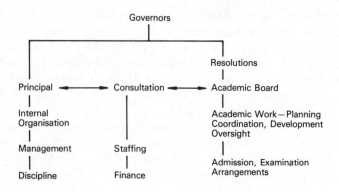

Fig. 3.4 Government at Richmond upon Thames College.

the climate of an institution. To achieve the aim of creating a college suited to the needs of the 16 to 19 year-old student means that the proportions of full-time post-19 students and part-time students must be carefully monitored. The full realisation of the tertiary concept depends on the careful coordination of the total curriculum. To achieve the maximum flexibility in the GCE A-level programme; to be able to integrate vocational and academic courses; to look after the most able and the least able: these are all part of this feature of the work of the academic board. Since in the college matrix system this aspect of the operation, together with the arrangements for admission and examination, is part of the management responsibility which the divisional directors hold, the initiation of course planning and coordination will probably be through them although individual members of staff have the opportunity to present their ideas to the board.

The development and oversight of the academic work of the college will incorporate a concern with teaching and learning techniques, the use and provision of teaching resources, in-service training and standards of performance. This area of management in the matrix system is the responsibility of the team leaders. To achieve a balance between staff and management representation on the academic board in a matrix organisation is difficult if the 'management' representation becomes too large. In Richmond upon Thames College a decision was made to include all team leaders and all directors which with a limited staff representation has resulted in a three-way balance between principals and directors, team leaders and others, as shown in Fig. 3.5.

This limitation in staff representation can only be regarded as satisfactory if the team leaders are identified as expressing staff views and if they ensure that they are consulting and informing their staff.

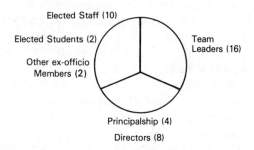

Fig. 3.5 The Academic Board of Richmond upon Thames College.

To keep the committee structure of the academic board small it was agreed that there should be three main sub-committees run under the chairmanship of the three assistant principals and aligned with their responsibilities. To these three a safety committee was added at an early stage. All the team leaders and all the directors are members of the curriculum committee; both have only one third non-management members. This particular balance is deliberately reversed in the environmental and student committee.

It is probably this feeling of imbalance both in the board itself and in two of its major committees that led to the demand for a standing committee composed mainly of elected members to act as a progress-chasing body and which can have more regular meetings with the principal in a way similar to that enjoyed by the team leaders and directors. Obviously the academic board had not created either the reality or the illusion of consultation and it is unlikely that the formation of another committee will have done much to improve this situation.

The Richmond upon Thames College governors exercise overall control of the institution in four ways which help to determine its character. First of all, the number of students is specified. This determines the scope and size of the buildings to be provided. For example for 2000 full-time students a communal area of 2000 square

metres is justified according to Department of Education and
Science standards. For this type of calculation the number of part-
time students is divided by five to give a daily average of full-time
equivalent students. Secondly, the curriculum is specified and
variations to the curriculum are made only on the advice of the
academic board and with the approval of the governors. Even in this
large broadly based college it is obvious that certain subject areas,
which demand expensive plant and where potential student numbers
are low, cannot be included. The target student enrolment for each
subject or course is part of the specification. The principal then
agrees with each student director the number of teaching hours
required by each group. This number of hours must allow for the
class to split for tutorial or option purposes or to allow for the introduction of large and small compensating teaching groups. Under
the new conditions of service a number of teaching equivalent hours
for pastoral resource or administrative duties, for example course
coordination, is set against each group and as a third step a total manpower budget is presented to the governors after consultation
with the academic board through the curriculum committee.

Each director is thus able to approach any team leader to service
his courses within an agreed proportion of this budget.

The fourth control is financial and is exercised through the college
estimates which are prepared by the principal in consultation with
the academic board and its resources committee. In the school
or sixth form college environment a single average capitation
allowance might be appropriate, but for a college with a wide
variation in type and level of course a more refined guide-line is
required. Calculations have shown that the estimate head for books,
stationery and materials needs to be drawn up assuming that the
needs of the craft student are a number of times greater than those of
the academic. The team leaders proportion of the budget is based on
the number of student hours and type of course taught by the
members of the team.

Ideas on organisation must in some way be linked with the
physical facilities. It is no good expecting a new organisation to work
if it is poured into old arrangements of classrooms and laboratories.
Very few colleges have ideal accommodation and inherit a variety of
buildings and, often, sites. If one accepts the premise of the 'new'
institution, then it must not be suggested by the physical layout that,

in the case of amalgamation, one component is absorbing the other or that, where a completely new college is planned, the organisation is predetermined. It is not just idiosyncracy or cussedness that rooms and laboratories are reallocated and renumbered. It is necessary to indicate that everyone is starting from scratch in a transformed situation. However, efficiency and morale may take some time to recover if this operation is not carried out with some care.

Once the organisation system has been determined, the building plan can follow. In the case of the matrix system an ideal layout would probably take the form of a wheel with the team areas at the end of the spokes and the hub containing communal and administrative facilities and staff concerned with the planning and coordination functions (see Fig. 3.6). Within the hub a balance must be achieved between open plan areas to encourage the maximum flexibility of operation between clerical and administrative sections and small offices where planning and interviewing including a careers and counselling service, can take place undisturbed. The concentration of the directors in the hub facilitates planning and

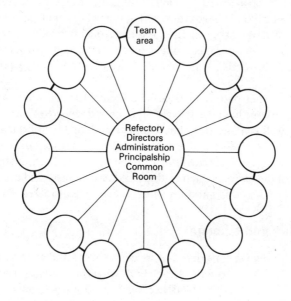

Fig. 3.6 The hub, spokes and rim of an organisational wheel.

coordination but limits their immediate assessment of client reaction in the classroom.

The provision of specialist facilities and names given to buildings will say something about the ethos of the institution. Without a sports hall, music and drama centre the development and encouragement of the performing arts is difficult. The provision of a library with adequate private study space shows the student that the college is orientated towards self-development and a concern for his individual study and learning needs. Communal facilities such as common rooms and refectories all determine the degree of social intermixing, both for staff and students.

Where new buildings are being designed it is possible to display the philosophy of the college. Are there possibilities for team teaching, rearranging furniture, open-plan working, use of film, or is one faced with standard battery classroom design with solid doors? There is no doubt too that students faced with a tidy, clean building attractively decorated will respond positively and vandalism will be less than in a building that is not maintained. Cognitive achievement is less likely to be affected by surroundings but expressive development is. The tertiary college is devoted to the 'whole man' concept of education and a well designed campus is therefore of great importance.

Such then is one organisational pattern constructed to match a defined need in terms of an inherited situation and the resources available.

Doubtless other patterns would be effective too. All that can be said is that this one has been tried in practice and seems to be working well. How well is a question that a college and/or Local Education Authority might wisely ask itself after some three sessions or so. Are there any changes of curriculum, the open-entry pattern, resource levels and organisation structure that need to be considered after an initial period? It is this question which is briefly considered finally.

Evaluation and Change

At the beginning we considered some of the needs and expectations involved in tertiary reorganisation. Following the formation of the college all those involved—consciously or not—will have been contributing to its climate and making some assessment of its impact and effectiveness.

Having introduced a pattern of organisation in a preliminary attempt to create a particular type of climate, we naturally want to ask whether it works. Many of the reactions, of course, will be subjective. Visitors have commented that Richmond upon Thames College is a lively, friendly establishment; others that the students appear to be working hard. To make a more objective assessment it would be necessary to use methods adopted by systematic investigators and obtain statistical information from both students and staff.[9]

Purely subjectively, it would appear that at Richmond upon Thames the team structure is providing for many of the staff needs. Feelings of insecurity exist still where external factors such as financial cuts and decrease in student enrolments mean that in certain courses the Local Education Authority is having to look at early retirement and redundancy schemes, but the general atmosphere is very positive. Subjectively also, students would appear to appreciate the freedoms and friendships which exist, and examination successes have been good in both the academic and vocational spheres.

It appears that horizontal communication between team leaders as a group, between directors as a group, and between members of the principalship, is good. Vertical communication patterns seem to be less satisfactory and this probably is the real test facing these three leadership groups in the matrix when compared with the departmental system. Only the future will tell.

Notes

1 Hutton, C. J., *Thinking about Organisation* (London, Tavistock Publications, 1972)
2 Musgrave, P. W., *The Sociology of Education* (London, Methuen, 1965)
3 Tannenbaum, A. S. and Smith, C. G., "Effects of Member Influence in Organisation, *Journal of Abnormal and Social Psychology,* 69(4) (1964), 9
4 Halpin, A. W., *Theory and Research in Administration* (New York, Collier Macmillan, 1966)
5 Dunham, J., 'Change and Stress in the Head of Departments' Role, *Journal of the National Foundation for Educational Research,* 21(1) (1978), 44 – 7

6   *Aspects of Comprehensive Education, Pastoral Care in Schools:* HMI report (London, DES, 1977), p.23
7   Musgrove, P., *The Family, Education and Society* (London, Routledge and Kegan Paul, 1966)
8   Bernstein, B., 'Open School, Open Society' *New Society* (14 Sept. 1967), 10 3513
9   Mohrman, A. M., (Jr.), Cooke, R. A., and Mohrman, S. A., 'Participation in Decision Making: A Multidimensional Perspective', *Educational Administration Quarterly* 14 (1) (1978)

4

THE 16 TO 19 CURRICULUM

E. W. Heley

The curriculum of a tertiary college is the curriculum on offer in the state system to an entire age group. It will have a strong local or regional component. The Boot and Shoe Industry courses at Accrington and Rossendale College would be inappropriate in Andover. Nevertheless, a comprehensive college must offer a complete range of courses which prepares young people for living in what is by international standards a small and fairly homogeneous country. The equality of opportunity so often thought of in class terms should not be neglected in geographical terms. National provision implies a national curriculum.

The tertiary college finds itself caught up in three major concerns of contemporary curriculum planning for the 16 to 19 age group, and in a fourth which it would not be too unfair to say is not of sufficient concern to the educational world. These are: the future of the traditional sixth form course; the problem of the 'new sixth'; the development of appropriate curricula in vocational education; and the neglected one, the education of the part-time student.

The first two of these have been considered until recently almost entirely in a school context. Until 'the great debate' was inaugurated by James Callaghan in 1976 the planning of the sixth form curriculum was the perogative of a Schools Council dominated by representative schoolteachers. The courses for the same age group in further education were never so teacher-oriented; indeed the licence of the one may be contrasted with the subservience of the other. The oppressive degree to which the programmes of further education have been dictated by outside bodies, some of which have little claim to educational expertise and whose narrowness of outlook and restrictive interpretation of education (usually expressed in overteaching and over-long incarceration for the student in class room, laboratory and workshop), has hindered the development of the college of further education as a corporate, cultured and ethical institution.

The tertiary college staff finds itself facing all of these problems, and many individuals discover themselves operating in all four fields. A former schoolteacher will be on a Business Education Council working party within his college. Here he will recoil from the apparent strait-jacket of a syllabus conceived in Skinnerian behavioural objectives and even regard it a training manual rather than a syllabus. A former grammar school English teacher may be asked to plan a communications unit for Level 1 of the Technical Education Council course. He cannot avoid consideration of the problem of relevance to the career actual or intended, of the student. In school the subject is king. The causes of the French Revolution, Shakespeare's imagery and the principles of optics do not have to justify their places in the curriculum on any external criterion of usefulness or relevance. On returning to his academic subject teaching in GCE A-level he find himself questioning the cafeteria system of study, the traditional content of subject teaching, and the lack of any integration between the heterogeneous elements of study.

Students, too, are able to compare and contrast the four regimes, particularly the first three—the sixth form, the new sixth, and the full-time vocational. According to disposition, the 'vocationals' envy or despise the shorter hours of class contact of GCE students and the amount of time they can devote to private study, sport or mere socialising. GCE students, particularly those whose subjects do not engage their intellects but are merely means to an end, become dissatisfied with a course of study which gives no help in choosing a career at 18. The one-year GCE O-level students (the 'new sixers') see their friends on one-year vocational courses with good job prospects, which in their case can only come from a success which is statistically unlikely.[1]

The tertiary college finds that what had hitherto been thought of as separate problems engaging the interest of quite unrelated bodies is in fact one—no less than the education of young people in the period between compulsory schooling and majority. The tertiary college could be organised as a loose federation of departments each with its own outlook, pastoral and care systems and educational assumptions and thus opt out of a holistic viewpoint. Fortunately parents will not allow this. They can understand the need for a wide range of courses to cater for the individual needs of their children but cannot accept (nor should they) the cavalier attitude to their existence characteristic of much further education. Once one college is the sole provider, a parent who may have several children passing through the system cannot agree to the 'ownership' of them by BEC or TEC or Joint Committee or whomsoever. They know that John and Mary have talents not necessarily completely catered for by a course in business studies however necessary the need to earn a living. It is not unreasonable to continue with music or a foreign language, and if the vocational courses do not make this possible then reluctantly perhaps, they will choose the GCE route.

For the sake of clarity the four elements are dealt with separately in what follows, but it must not be forgotten that courses are but a means to an end. Young people do not divide themselves up into convenient 'target groups'. The 'hidden curriculum', a euphemism for what a school really teaches, must not promote the view that all courses (and students) are equal but some . . .

The Traditional Sixth Form

The traditional sixth form course has become a cramming in two or three subjects and very little else. General Studies or minority time, or whatever unexamined study is called, is often a facade. The young see no reason to give time or energy to such parts of their course. They know that university places are given to those with good grades in specialist subjects and they are unwilling to risk

their futures in the interest of a liberal education. As A. D. C.
Peterson wrote in 1973:

> It has been pointed out again and again that what universities say,
> which is that they want broadly educated sixth-formers, conflicts with
> what they actually do, which is to allot the coveted places to those who
> do best in their specialised subjects irrespective of their general
> education.[2]

This fact, known to staff and student alike, inhibits both from
wholehearted commitment to a broader curriculum. In *The Sixth
Form and its Alternatives,* an NFER report published in 1979, there
are no less than five pages of students' comments on the variously
named, general, elective, recreative, and minority studies, and they
are almost universally hostile. Some express views that are frankly
philistine: 'I think too much importance is placed on giving us a
general education, i.e. core studies' (yet another euphemism); 'If
we want to learn about these sorts of things we can do without
being forced to listen to a teacher lecturing on what he wants to.
We come to school really, to study for exams.'[3] (This from a
grammar school pupil.) Aspiring parents, pot-hunting schools, or
both, have done their worst.

Some young people were more constructive, suggesting that
General Studies should be relevant to their future as citizens.
Courses in law, personal relations, mortgages, politics or practical
skills had their advocates, but even those who were examined in
General Studies were less than enthusiastic. We cannot expect the
young to make suggestions for improving the sixth form
curriculum when they do not have the experience of the broad
human education which alone would make it possible for them to
do so.

Every proposal for reform of the sixth form curriculum has been
shipwrecked on the shores of academic obscurantism and the reefs
of vested interest. The universities have consistently demanded that
sixth-formers be prepared for a degree course specialism, quite
ignoring the fact that only a minority of traditional sixth-formers
go up to university. The excuse given is the shortness of the British
first-degree course and the necessity of covering in the schools
much of the work that would be done in the first year at university
on the continent or in the USA. Some sixth form teachers, perhaps
flattered by an assumption of vicarious university status, defend

their subjects against the attack of generalists and balanced curriculum-mongers in terms of scholarship, excellence and the maintenance of standards.

One needs to ask: what excellence, what standards? We have science graduates whose knowledge of the arts and social sciences is no higher than O-level, and there are arts graduates who pride themselves on knowing nothing of science, technology or mathematics, and since neither group will have received an education beyond the third year in practical skills, both can despise the craftsman and the technician who never had a sixth form education at all.

The interest now being shown in the International Baccalaureate[4] by some tertiary colleges is due to its insistence on a compulsory spread of study expressed in six basic elements. These are the language of instruction (English in the United Kingdom), another language, Science, Mathematics, Study of Man (History, Economics and so on), and an optional choice. Aesthetic, artistic or practical studies are compulsory and earn credit, and the whole is given coherence by a course in the theory of knowledge. The resulting programme is one that demands of the able an open and enquiring attitude to a broad spectrum of knowledge and prohibits too early a commitment to a speciality.

It is not the purpose of this book to advocate the International Baccalaureate which suffers from being unjustly perceived as a broad education for linguists rather than a balanced sixth form curriculum for everyone. Educationists might note that it has the advantage of being a course rather than an assemblage of separate subjects. Further education teachers will need no persuading on this score. It keeps alive science and mathematics among arts students and social sciences and languages (including their own) among scientists and insists on an aesthetic and philosophic education for all of them. It may not be the sixth form education we have been looking for, but few can doubt it to be a good deal more balanced than the narrowly based GCE A-level model even where this is still eked out with unrelated, unexamined and low-status 'minority time'. Even worse than these is the misuse of GCE O-level and the Certificate of Extended Education as a topping-up. The first is often otiose, mere wolf-cub badge collections. The CEE is intended for an entirely different target group (CSE 2 – 4 at 16).

The course is warped by the presence of high-flyers to the detriment of those for whom it as designed.

The amount of time devoted in academic boards and teachers' conferences to General Studies is not evidence of a healthy interest, more a sign of despair at the difference between the myth and the reality. As Peterson[5] has shown, the myth suggests that sixth-formers spend up to three-quarters of their time on their GCE A-level subjects and one quarters on what the Crowther report called in 1959 minority time. Yet, as he points out, nearly half of all sixth-formers in 1967 were taking no general studies other than physical education and religion. The situation is hardly likely to have improved in the meantime. Sixth-formers in a college of further education are not obliged by law to study religion, while in schools compulsory religion is seen as counterproductive by those who are religious and as an impertinence by those who are not.

The tertiary college cannot claim to have solved the problem. It could not do so in isolation. Its students cannot move too far from the normal sixth form experience if they are to be successful in the race for places in higher education or employment. Yet it can achieve some broadening of the curriculum within present constraints. Its greatest contribution so far is extra-curricular and social. Meeting and having to take account of the views and needs of students committed to careers or already in work are features of sixth form education uniquely tertiary.

The small school sixth form and many further education colleges make it difficult for the student to choose GCE A-levels from across the spectrum and even more difficult to combine GCE work with other courses. The notion of the 'arts sixth' and the 'science sixth' may be kept alive in the small sixth form more by timetabling difficulties than a philosophical position. In colleges of further education the autonomous department may hinder free student choice. (The view that buildings have dictated the development of English education is well illustrated in the further education department. Although originating in a thousand scattered annexes, old schools and halls, it has survived intact in the purpose-built college.)

The tertiary college offers a programme of GCE studies. Departments serve the programme, not vice versa. A college timetable becomes essential. It is not necessary for some polymath

	0900	1000	1100	1200	1300	1400	1500	1600	1700	Staff Available for Meetings	Evening Programme
Monday	3	3	3	5	5	(5)	1	1	1	5	E.P.
Tuesday	4	4	4	Divisional Hour (Tutorials, Assemblies)	2	(2)	5	5	5	4	E.P.
Wednesday	1	1	1	3	3	(3)	4	4	4	3	E.P.
Thursday	5	5	5	1	1	(1)	3	3	3	2	E.P.
Friday	2	2	2	4	4	(4)	2	2	2	2	E.P.

Lunch Period
(these hours are alternatives)

Fig. 4.1 Allocation of modules in the week. GCE A-level subjects have five hours, GCE O-level/CEE have four hours. Within a seven-hour module various arrangements are possible—long blocks of time or more frequent meetings of short duration. Three TEC units can be accommodated in each module. Fully integrated courses such as Private Secretaries Certificate, TEC Diploma, DATEC Diploma (1 year) need only keep modular time for creative (general) studies.

Module 1 (6 hrs)	Module 2 (6 hrs)	Module 3 (7 hrs)	Module 4 (7 hrs)	Module 5 (7 hrs)
English RSA CEE O A English as a foreign lang.	Maths RSA CEE O A	English RSA CEE O A	Maths RSA CEE O A	English RSA CEE O A English as a foreign lang.
	(This is a stacked programme. Students take appropriate level of literacy/numeracy)			
A-Level	A-Level	A-Level	A-Level	A-Level
A/O-Levels	A/O-Levels	A/O-Levels	A/O-Levels	A/O-Levels
	(Students choose one or two as supportive study)			
O-Levels CEE	O-Levels CEE	O-Levels CEE	O-Levels CEE	O-Levels CEE
	May be combined with A-Level/AO/TEC etc.			
◄──── DATEC Diploma ────►			Choice	Choice
Choice	Choice	Choice	Shorthand	Typewriting
◄──── OND (Technology) ────►				Choice
Choice	◄──── BEC National Award ────►			
◄──── TEC/BEC General Certificate ────►			Choice	Choice
Creative Studies Sport Movement Drama Music etc.	Creative Studies Archaeology Motor – Maintenance Community – Service etc.	Creative Studies Sailing Photography Choir etc.	Creative Studies Representative– Sport Languages Pottery etc.	Creative Studies Orchestra Painting Newspaper etc.

Fig. 4.2 An integrated college timetable. Students choose one element from each module.

armed with a computer to arrange every detail. A simple modular structure is imposed—the details are delegated. A matrix management system makes it easier to adopt the policy but is not essential to its success. One version is shown in Figs. 4.1 and 4.2. This is a five-modular system allowing for three GCE A-levels, a module for other studies and a module for private and social life. It also allows for five GCE O-levels or CEE subjects, or any combination up to five component parts. Models based on other numbers of modules are possible, but in a 30 hour week the number of hours per module may become too low for subjects with a practical component, like Nuffield Physics. The large number of students in the subjects currently leading the field enables a tertiary college to place at least once class of reasonable size in each module. This ensures that a student can combine two of these with subjects that appear on the list only once. In this way a tertiary college can keep alive subjects which are disappearing from smaller institutions. It would be a very small education district which could not support one class in GCE A-level Latin. Further, the college can have reasonable groups in subjects which are often not on offer at all such as Russian, Design and Technology, and Religion. One young man known to us whose ambition was to enter the Anglican ministry attended a grammar school whose sixth form curriculum did not include religious studies. He made his way to the civic centre of his borough and was told that in the whole authority, mainly comprehensively organised and boasting a large further education college, there was nowhere offering GCE A-level Religious Studies. He was directed to the only tertiary college in London. 'Free trade' made this possible. We have since heard that one school in that LEA is now offering the subject, perhaps a response to a quip about their being godless!

One of the unresolved dilemmas in the tertiary college is in the education of the most able. The further education tradition is firmly against streaming.

The school sixth form is lucky to have a viable group in all but a handful of popular subjects so that the problem hardly arises. For a tertiary college both the temptation and the opportunity are great. Richmond upon Thames College has no less than ten groups of 10–15 students in each year studying GCE A-level English. Most of these are in the nature of things taking the subject as one of three; their main interest lies in some other subject. There are however a considerable number of students whose ambition is to read English at university or for whom it is a particular interest and not a means to an end. The temptation to earmark (say) module 3 English for the latter group is very strong. In Mathematics this kind of streaming has to be done so that the dedicated mathematicians can be free to take Further Mathematics, a subject which appears once only. It would be idle to pretend that the colleges have resolved this conflict of ethos. Our own view is that the college's duty is to the individual student. The most able in our community are a precious national resource. Their education and welfare cannot be sacrificed to some notion of general good. Such policies are always self-defeating. Yet the self-fulfilling prophecy effect of streaming described by Hargreaves[6] and many others—that those labelled C stream accept the grading and adjust their achievements to the classification—is so well attested that to proceed along that path is to put at risk the fundamental ethos of the tertiary college. There is a way out of the dilemma—individualised, resource-based learning which ensures that all students are allowed to proceed at their own learning pace. As Denis Lawton has commented, 'very able pupils are not held back to a false norm of an A stream class'.[7] For this mode of learning to be a real possibility the institution must have a library that is not a mere repository of books but central to the whole educational process (see Essay 8).

Class teaching along traditional lines there will be, and we must console ourselves with the thought that in mixed-ability classes the cooperative impulse can be given its due in a competitive examination-oriented system.

The New Vocational Sixth Form

This heading may occasion some surprise. We are accustomed to sixth-formers whose subjects are pure and those of roughly equal ability who follow National Diploma standard courses at colleges of further education and are certainly not usually regarded as sixth-formers. In a tertiary college this distinction based on institutions rather than educational values seems unwarranted.

If the further education courses are timetabled in the college modular system, as described above, then it becomes possible for a student to combine elements from both GCE and vocational studies into one sensible comprehensive package. There are problems. These have little to do with genuine difficulty but a great deal to do with unrealistic attitudes and the splendid isolationism of those responsible for setting up vocational programmes. Doubtless it will take time to break down barriers, but for the tertiary college it is essential that artificial constraints be removed.

The kind of combinations which are possible may be illustrated from the 'hybrids' currently offered at Richmond upon Thames College. This college inherited from its college of technology component a thriving department of Art and Design, ranging from foundation level to advanced vocational design leading to the Society of Industrial Artists and Designers Diploma. Art and Design education is being restructured into a 2 + 2 format very roughly corresponding to the OND, HND form long familiar in Engineering and Business education. It is possible to meet the requirements of the lower level (to be known as DATEC Diploma) in approximately three-fifths of the instructional time over two years, or about 15 hours per week. If this is timetabled in the college modules taking up two and part of a third, the remaining two modules may be used for any subject in the list and at any level. Students have opted for GCE A-level subjects as academic as History and English Literature, where of course they are taught in the same classes as students on a full GCE programme. Other students choose GCE A-level subjects with particular relevance to their Art and Design course, such as Photography, Design and Technology or, with a different emphasis, Drama. Many take one of each kind. Since they can take GCE A-level Art or History of Art in their stride successful students end their time at college qualified for degree courses in Fine Art or vocational courses in Art and Design, or may decide that they have extended their formal visual education long enough and transfer to more academic programmes at 18 + .

The BEC National Diploma or OND in Technology can be covered in four modules. This enables students able and willing to take a language or Mathematics at A-level. Shorthand and Typewriting at a high level of competence can be combined with two A-levels, giving students a choice of options at 18 and affording excellent career prospects. London employers seem to have no qualms about offering good employment to students qualified to RSA III levels in skills and GCE A-level in English (AEB) and Economics (London). So far not one has been asked 'Have you got your PSC?'[8] Others have gone to university or polytechnic where they are no doubt using shorthand to take notes and their portables to transcribe them—possibly for the boyfriend too!

Richmond upon Thames College is becoming almost embarrassed by the large number of applications for hybrid courses of this kind. Traditionalists among its further education staff are worried about the weakening effect it may have on the benefits of the integrated approach, while former school sector colleagues have worries which are a mirror image. Perhaps these students will lack the full commitment to an academic discipline and be too obviously career-motivated. It is our belief that such fears will prove as groundless as most educational bogeys arising from resistance to change. We note that in the Land of North-Rhine-Westphalia, tertiary colleges, known with German logic as *Kollegschule,* are promoted on the basis of double qualification. Parents receive a colour brochure in which preternaturally well groomed youngsters boast of gaining 'Abitur' and a technical qualification.[9] We must consider very carefully whether we want our youth in full-time education to commit themselves to narrow career objectives at 16, based on almost complete ignorance of the employment market, insufficient careers advice (a national scandal), and incomplete self-knowledge. The types of programme outlined in this section have at least the merit of maintaining choice until 18 + .

Students on these double qualification courses are a force for integration in the college. Moving freely as they do between vocational departments and academic ones, they subtly change the atmosphere in both, perhaps, in so doing, tending to confirm the suspicions already mentioned. Those who share with the authors of this book a scepticism of the behavioural objectives approach adopted by the Technician and Business Education Councils and an unwillingness to regard Bloom[10] as the last word on the aims of education may be pleased that these double-qualification students are exposed to an older and more liberal tradition.

The 'New Sixth'

In Essay 2 the nature and origins of the 'new sixth' have been discussed, and it would be true to say that the continuative full-time education for one further year of this large and growing group of young people of average ability has not been put on a sound basis. The school offers more of the same; often humiliatingly, by repeating a year with the fifth form. The college of further education offers GCE O-level repeats too, but with the incentive that the boy or girl will be treated as an adult. Alternatively the colleges have pressed into full-time service courses originally designed for the part-time student already at work. For example, until the early 1970s the Certificate of Office Studies, now replaced by the BEC General Diploma, was a part-time course.[11] It was with evident reluctance that the Joint Committee at the Department of Education and Science bowed to teacher pressure and allowed COS to become a full-time equivalent course. Its reluctance was understandable. As with all courses of this kind, including those of the City and Guilds, the knowledge and attitudes gained from work experience could be taken for granted and form a valuable if unstated part of the whole concept. Stretched to cover the week and deprived of the nourishment of actual application to work, the course fulfilled neither the objectives of a vocational education nor those of a liberal one. Colleges were enjoined to simulate work experience—something easier said than done—and to ensure participation by the student in an enrichment programme of General Studies. If General Studies have little appeal for the intelligentsia among students, it is hardly surprising that their appeal to average students is less than overwhelming.

The growth of the further education 'new sixth' has brought a flurry of curriculum planning during the decade, the most notable being the programmes of the Technician and Business Education Councils, the City and Guilds Institute and the Royal Society of Arts. Several other bodies have been active also. Six Regional Examining Bodies for Further Education prepared schemes for a Certificate of Further Education either on an inter-regional or separate basis. Following the Schools' Council *Working Paper 45* of 1972, the CSE Examining Boards have promoted pilot schemes in the Certificate of Extended Education. These have been taken up enthusiastically by many sixth form colleges for they have sufficient one-year students to make up economically sized teaching groups. The CEE has been less popular among 11 to 18 schools, especially small ones. Despite cross-moderation exercises, the format of these examinations, the type of subject offered, the ability range of candidates, standards of marking and grade of awards has shown a degree of variation which strains credibility. This is particularly unfortunate since CEE grades 1, 2 and 3 are linked to CSE 1 and this in turn is the equivalent of GCE O-level C grade—or the former minimum pass level.

To have a second-rate GCE O-level pass (CSE 1) is demeaning enough—to have a third-rate one is ludicrous, as the Keohane Report[12] tacitly admits. Indeed, it recommends that CEE be 'free-standing'.

Enough has been said to give the reader some idea of the scale and range of curricula currently being offered or proposed for those in one year of full-time education beyond the statutory leaving age.

The basic problem is that the one examination which enjoys an established reputation is the GCE O-level. It is cash in a credit card world. Parents press for it. Employers express their recruitment policy in its terms as if ability to pass some four or five school subjects in a sudden-death examination told them anything very vital about their recruits—save an ability to pass four or five school subjects in a sudden-death examination. We have to put up with the ignorance that demands O-level Mathematics for work that needs at best accuracy in the simpler form of arithmetic. No less annoying is the preference shown to those with GCE O-level certificates at D grade (formerly the highest form of failure) to CSE Grade 1 applicants. The CSE has had to endure the gibe that it is a certificate of second-class education from those who do not understand that the GCE was intended only for the top 20 per cent of the ability range at 16 + . Clearly some of the 17-year-old students will be able to convert CSE or O-levels below C to the desired GCE O-level at grades A – C, but the proportion is low. The task of persuading the young people of this, still more their parents, is a difficult one. It is not helped if the alternatives have neither currency nor attractiveness. One of the objectives the London Borough of Richmond upon Thames in setting up its tertiary college was to put a limit to the growth of GCE O-level repeats and CSE conversion courses, which had doubled in its two sixth form colleges after reorganisation in 1973. It was hoped that in the tertiary college young people would opt for a wide variety of educational programmes leading to qualifications which enhanced their employment prospects. While we note an encouraging increase in the number of young people engaged on such vocational courses compared with the former further education institutions, the diminution in the number of students on GCE O-level courses has been only marginal. What has happened is that the 'staying on' rate has gone up and the extra students are, as is inevitable in an area such as Richmond, in the lower levels of ability. (In areas with low staying on rates and high unemployment levels a high proportion of young people of ability leave school at 16. In south-east England the proportion of high-ability stayers-on is so great that any increase in the rate increases the number of average and below-average students disproportionately.) Since there are sometimes good reasons for failure at 16, illness, puberty, removal, parental discord, bereavement, as well as poor schooling (only in 'public relations' are all 11 to 16 schools equally good), a GCE O-level course is essential. The three-year sixth form is now a common experience. GCE O-level subjects have to be in the programme of many GCE A-level students to plug gaps. Regrettably many young people have insufficient scientific background or are short of a modern language. Latin, Chemistry and Physics must be offered from scratch if able students are to have full opportunities in higher education. It is clear, however, that GCE O-level study over one year is not an ideal course for those who have been educated in the very different style of the CSE. The obvious answer is the CEE. This is operated by the same examining boards. The curricula are arrived at by practising teachers and not imposed by the board. Whatever the differences already mentioned, all the pilot schemes emphasise the student's own participation. In the South East Region for example, only one third of the marks are for the common core examination. The other two-thirds are given for two teacher-assessed optional areas of study. Although the examination is available in colleges of further education, it has been almost completely ignored there. The reason, apart from school/FE particularism, is that it is not self-evident that the ideal course of study for the 17 year-old is more of the same: five separate 'school' subjects none of which is vocational and few of any direct relevance to the life, needs, or even the cultural aspirations of the student. It is damned in further education terms for not being a course. The esprit de corps among students on even the least prestigious further education course may come as a surprise to some. The college of further education is surely right to doubt if an *à la carte* menu, an atomic existence and an absence of a central integrating study can be right for young people of average ability straight from school. Sophisticated pastoral case systems and elaborate tutorial organisation are no substitute for a coherent group working under the guidance of a small number of staff who work together to plan, execute, teach and learn. For this reason the Certificate of Further Education is offered in some areas, according to an NFER report, 'to help students who have been unable to decide on a future career while still at school or whose examination results have proved unsatisfactory to themselves and prospective employers'[13]. The forms of the CFE vary but all emphasise a common core of numeracy, communication skills and social skills. There are 33 vocational modules currently offered in the Union of Educational Institutions scheme, a student chooses two. No college offers the full range. Teachers are quoted in the NFER report, an interim one, as being agreed that students derive benefit from the course, though as is usual in education they do not agree about the nature of the benefit.

Some colleges offer City and Guilds Foundation Courses. These are very similar to the Certificate of Further Education Courses except that each one is more narrowly devoted to a particular job. One of the problems about all of these courses, whether CEE, CFE, Foundation C&G, is that when the student is 17 he may not be as acceptable for apprenticeship as a 16 year-old with similar qualifications. This is so true of the vocational Foundation Courses that these are best confined to schools and followed in the fourth and fifth years.

Is the new sixth doomed then to studies which are either irrelevantly academic with scant chance of success or relevantly vocational with no guarantee of a job. Fortunately, we do not have to choose either. The study group set up to consider the future (if any) of the Certificate of Extended Education under the chairmanship of Professor Keohane has produced a report which is a model of clarity and good sense. The report, *Proposals for a Certificate of Extended Education,* has not heeded the siren voices asking for a continuation of a sixth form course based on school subjects in the narrowest sense:

'It appears that over two-thirds of those taking the CEE pilot examinations expect to seek employment on completing their studies at 17 + . It is therefore crucial that CEE, if it is to be officially introduced, should be able to prepare young people effectively for employment. Many of the young people concerned now take or re-take GCE O-levels or CSEs. Whilst this may be appropriate in some cases, these examinations are in general inappropriate and may have the disadvantage of representing 'last year's work' and of being designed primarily for younger pupils. There is therefore a clear case for a course leading to a different examination for the young people concerned. But if this is to satisfy the needs of those going straight into employment it must be capable of ensuring basic communication and numerical skills, providing some element of vocational preparation, assisting in the development of personal and social skills relevant to work, and offering certification which gives assurance to employers on these points. The Schools Council's proposals for a CEE do not adequately satisfy these requirements and we recommend a number of changes to their proposals.[14]

The report goes on to recommend that communications (including oral) and numeracy should be a compulsory element in all CEE certificates. Since at the moment a single CEE subject can be taken as part of a package of GCE subjects at various levels, this requirement clearly implies that CEE should become a grouped course. Keohane's report does not go this far. It does however add:

Schools and colleges should also use the flexibility afforded by the single subject approach to examining to develop grouped courses including the elements seen as important by employment interests . . . using linked arrangements and work experience when necessary.[15]

The relevance of this to tertiary colleges is clear. They alone have all the new sixth. As further education institutions they are in touch with employers on a regular basis. They can plan that integration of further education courses and the CEE that Keohane insists is desirable. If the report of the study group established by the Board of Management of the Further Education Curriculum Review and Development Unit is implemented then the CEE, CFE and other courses will become very similar, each in the words of Keohane 'emphasing a broad education deriving from the common demand made on young people as adult citizens and workers'.[16] Keohane believes that linking the two types of course will give both greater currency if they related to a single national scheme. This would require 'encouragement (of) closer collaboration between schools and colleges of further education'.[17]

Such cooperation is much more likely to occur within tertiary colleges than between separate institutions. The Keohane study group has called for a comprehensive approach to the educational provision for the one-year sixth-former. Organisation was outside the terms of reference, but comprehensive provision can best be forwarded in a comprehensive institution—the tertiary college.

Full-time Vocational Courses

In discussing the 'new sixth' we have thought it more sensible to include in that term all young people extending their full-time education by one year. There can be little point in a separate discussion based on the historical accident that some are in schools and some in further education. In this section attention is drawn therefore mainly to the alternatives to GCE A-level and other vocational courses which last longer than one year.

Students with four GCE O-level passes can enter National Diploma courses at the local college of further education. The most prestigious of these is the Ordinary National Diploma (Technology). The four O-level entry for this must include Mathematics, Physics or an acceptable scientific alternative, and at least one subject in which facility in English is shown. The course is rather theoretical and is very demanding in time and hard work. Controlled by a Joint Committee at the Department of Education and Science in which professional bodies are represented the diploma is recognised by the Engineering Institutions as a step on the road to Chartered Engineer status. Universities and polytechnics accept a high-level pass for degree courses and the normal pass is acceptable for entry to the Higher National Diploma—a technician engineer qualification. In an industrial society, one would be forgiven for thinking that queues would be forming to obtain a place on the course. The reality is very different. The number of students on National Diploma programmes remains disappointingly small. The proposal to transfer the whole course to the Technician Education Council seems to many to set a limit to the possibility of changing this. The other National Diploma programmes have already been transferred to TEC and BEC.

The basis of the TEC programme is one of progression from a relatively low level of attainment at 16+ (CSE3, the average national attainment) to the highest possible an individual can reach at a speed, if not individualised at least that of his group. The technical studies are broken down into units with a numerical value depending on difficulty and duration. There are three levels each requiring five units for a pass. Thus 15 units are required for a certificate; a student gaining 25 units is awarded a diploma. The mode of attendance is not mandatory. It is quite common to take levels one and two by full-time study and the third by day release after finding a job. Some youngsters are on such programmes by courtesy of the Engineering Industry Training Board and the college full-time year is both off-the-job training and further education. Such students are paid and have jobs ready for them on completing the full-time year. Unfortunately the Industry Training Boards cannot be persuaded to allow these students to be treated as the other full-time students. Their working day is regulated and as long as in industry. In a tertiary college with its talented 'sixth form' enjoying a superabundance of activities and even fun, this deprivation is the more acutely felt. As one intelligent student at Richmond upon Thames College has commented:

> The TEC Instrumentation course has a good balance of practical work and classroom theory. The week is 35 hours long with no free periods for private study; this is a drawback. Lectures are usually of two hours duration and by the end of the period interest is waning. The lectures should be shorter and then interest could be maintained.

Craft courses in appropriate trades for its locality are also a feature of most tertiary colleges. These are usually sponsored by Industry Training Boards. It is not generally a good idea to learn a trade speculatively. A young craftsman with no employment to go to would have been better off had he taken a more general course.

Business education below degree level is now organised by the Business Education Council. There are two courses for the 16 to 18 age group. For the less able or those wanting only one year of study there is a 'craft' level called BEC General Diploma. For those who have obtained a credit level general diploma or who have four GCE O-levels on entry there is the BEC National Diploma. The former is a good course, popular with students and staff. It is designed to meet the criticism of the former Certificate in Office Studies made earlier in this chapter. As with all BEC courses, the approach is an integrated one, following through business problems which seldom present themselves in the real world in terms of law or accounts or whatever. The BEC National Diploma, which replaces the OND (Business Studies), is also based on core studies with individual cross-modular assignments as a most important teaching method. Staff used to isolated working within disciplines have found the need to work together and rethink their philosophy and methodology most stimulating. It is fortunate for tertiary colleges that these new structures have made it easier to involve former schoolteachers in vocational work where their pedagogic professionalism has been brought to bear with encouraging results.

The Haslegrave revolution[18] is now being applied to Art and Design education through an off-shoot of TEC known as DATEC (Design and Art TEC). It is too early to say what effect this will have on curricula but already the same ferment of activity and welding of former GCE A-level Art teachers and vocational art teachers into an effective team is occurring.

It is a pity that TEC is so bureaucratic. The forests of the world do not deserve to be decimated to make so many computer print-outs of information which could just as well be in a traditional mark book. Staff ask for time to do administrative clerical work which would be more sensibly used in class contact and tutoring. BEC has, even more than TEC, and much less appropriately, completely adopted the language (jargon?) of the behaviourist school. Fortunately most staff learn to use the jargon but to teach within wider objectives. Yet it is worrying. Vocational courses in tertiary colleges are so many and varied, serving so many local industries and businesses, that it is impossible to list them all. Keohane wisely suggests we need a national scheme with local mode III options of a vocational stamp, in place of so many full-time courses which are bewildering to the prospective student and often a complete mystery to employers.

The Part-time Student

As we have seen in Essay 2 the history of day release in Britain is a sorry one. The majority of young people in this country cease to have any connection with the education system once they leave school. Enlightened industries recognise the importance of an educated work force as distinct from a trained one. The former is flexible and retrainable; the latter often inflexible and a brake on change and development. The need for young people—and not only the young—to be educated for flexibility and retrainability is nowhere better illustrated than in the statistics for job-loss between 1970 – 75 in industries subject to competition from Third World countries. Surprisingly for those addicted to import controls, the figures show that half the job loss was due to increased productivity, which is another way of saying technological change:[19]

Reasons for lost jobs in 24 industries most affected by Third World competition, 1970—75.

Falling home demand	52 800
Rising productivity at home	214 300
Falling exports to Non Third World countries	20 800
Rising imports from Non Third World countries	92 600
Falling exports to Third World countries	800
Rising imports from Third World countries	47 000
	428 300

The extension of part-time education is more likely to come as a response to intolerable youth unemployment than as a progressive measure in its own right. Day release would increase the number of vacancies for those aged 16 to 18 by 20 per cent in those industries where it is not currently being offered, or alternatively it would enable firms to cut their youth employment by the same percentage without adding to unemployment totals.

As far as further education including tertiary colleges is concerned, there is much to be said for block release rather than day release. Students on day release have no time available for savouring the benefits of a college education. Many spend the whole day and evening in classrooms and workshops. The only facility of a college they use is the canteen, where their liberality with spending money contrasts with the tea and biscuits of the full-time student. As we have already noted, the day release student is usually male and has precious little time for discussion or getting to know students of both sexes on other courses. The block release student gets away from the place of work and may be seen in the library, common room, or sports hall. He becomes a temporary full-time student. In educational terms too, the concentrated period of study yields more dividends than day study interspersed by the cares and concerns of the workplace.

The further education sector is not blameless in the case of the part-time student. He is often given substandard accommodation in annexes and the oldest parts of the campus. His needs are overlooked, not least by student organisations run by full-timers. One of the problems is the ridiculously low value placed on the part-time student in terms of Burnham points. The part-timer takes at least as long as a full-timer to recruit. His course is as demanding in preparation time. He sits examinations which are as time-consuming to prepare as those of the full-timer. Marking is as onerous. Records (particularly those of TEC) are as complicated. A further education department finding that one full-time student is as valuable in salary and resource terms as three part-time students, at the most favourable parity, will settle if it can for the easy option: no visits to firms, no training officers to placate. A tertiary college with its guaranteed full-time student population is particularly at risk. It must make a conscious effort to recognise its duty to all young people, and not only those who continue in full-time education. Beyond this it awaits a government with the courage and vision to implement an idea that was not new when it appeared in the 1918 Education Act.

Advanced Courses (Post—18)

Most of the tertiary colleges have little or no work for post-18 students. Richmond upon Thames College is exceptional in this respect since its further education component was a college of technology. It has Higher National Diplomas in Engineering and Business Studies, Advanced Vocational Design, and high-level Secretarial Studies. These full-time courses fit naturally onto the 16 to 18 provision, particularly in the design field where it is usual for Foundation and Advanced work in Art and Design to be in the same institution.

As this aspect of the Richmond upon Thames College is unusual, somewhat controversial, and not essential to the argument of this book, we would make only one point. The flight of many of the polytechnics from part-time advanced vocational education has been one of the dismal regressions of the last 20 years. It is essential to preserve in the post-compulsory system the ability to progress to TEC higher certificates (formerly HNC) and through supplementary subjects to Technician Engineer status, by part-time study. If this exists in a tertiary college is would be wanton educational vandalism to end it by applying too restrictive a definition of tertiary.

The recent *Educational Credit Transfer Feasibility Study* (known as the Toyne Report) published in November 1979 is relevant to a tertiary college with a wide spectrum of courses.[21] One of the casualties of the plethora of courses available in the British education scene is the student who either leaves a course before completion or wishes to transfer to another. Institutions have little information on comparability. The easiest thing to do is to give no credit for past study and insist on an applicant repeating those elements common to both his previous and his intended course. Not surprisingly this leads to a considerable if unquantifiable withdrawal from education.

Universities are finding that no less than 15 per cent of applications and 11 per cent of admissions are from applicants offering alternative qualifications to GCE A-level. Some 6 per cent of applicants have 'advanced standing'. That is, they already have qualifications which include some elements of the degree they wish to read. Most of these are probably Higher National Diploma students. Polytechnics and other higher education institutions have a higher proportion of applicants with qualifications other than GCE. As the shortened version of the report says:

> A very wide variety of different educational opportunities in Higher and Further Education exists in the UK and there is an increasingly wide variety in the number of qualificational and experiential routeways by which access to those opportunities may be secured. Practices, however, tend to vary between institutions in terms of their entry requirements and attitudes to alternative qualifications and transfer with advanced standing.[22]

As tertiary organisation becomes more common the numbers of students opting for varied 'qualificational and experiential routeways' will increase. For this reason we welcome the setting up of a national system of information on credit transferability. The Open University, the Council for National Academic Awards

(CNAA) the City & Guilds, BEC and TEC have agreed on the need; the first two have already a credit transferability agreement.

In a survey of students who did not complete a course:

> as many as 45.5 per cent of the responding students were not in possession of information which might have assisted them to transfer to another course. Instead they discontinued their education.[23]

The report takes note of the greater flexibility which is developing both in modes of study and types of educational access nd draws attention to the need to review admission procedures to allow for experiential learning, alternative qualification and greater provision for advanced standing. Do we, however, hear once again the voice of the élitist establishment in the statement in the report:

> The need for (the scheme) to remain advisory and in no way to encroach on the autonomy of individual institutions has been stressed.[24]

Later in the decade there will be a falling off in the number of 18 year-old students. Perhaps even the universities might then find autonomy on entrance expressed in ever lower GCE A-level grades too dearly bought while students with alternative qualifications will be using their credits to keep up numbers in the polytechnics and institutions of higher education.

The Hidden Curriculum

> The question of all questions for humanity, the problem which lies behind all others and is more interesting than any of them is that of the determination of man's place in Nature and his relation to the Cosmos. Whence our race came, what sorts of limits are set to our power over Nature and to Nature's power over us, to what goal are we striving, are the problems which present themselves afresh, with undiminished interest to every human being born on earth.[20]

So wrote T. H. Huxley in 1863. We may, perhaps a little unfairly, compare this view of man's intellectual quest with those of the grammar school sixth-former quoted earlier in which the true purpose of education is to pass examinations. The most unfortunate effect of our national obsession with examinations is the biasing of the learning process towards topics which lend themselves to testing methods or the formulation of questions which have right answers. This deadening hand robs learning and enquiry of intellectual excitement, reduces aesthetic appreciation to priggish second-hand assessments, and devalues the brain-hand-eye combination which is the origin of our unique human intelligence. Writing about skills is no guarantee of proficiency. The normal tenor of instruction is literary with the end in view of composing under stressful conditions that most difficult and archaic of literary forms, the essay. Multiple-choice questions have been introduced in some examinations to kill two educational birds with one stone. They deal with the problem that only a few topics from a syllabus can be tested by essay, thus giving an unfair advantage to students whose teachers are experienced at spotting questions. It also copes with that perennial difficulty, the well written answer, thin in content, gaining credit over a bald narrative that goes to the heart of the matter. Unfortunately we are now out of the 'literary' fire and into the 'collection-of-facts' frying pan. Education is not about facts, but ideas. It is also about increasing and social competence—personal, social, practical and intellectual. We are good at testing the acquisition of facts. We have striven to find ways of examining the student's handling of ideas, and practical tests are probably the most objective of all our examinations. But we have failed utterly to devise any sensible means of examining personal and social competence, though one suspects that any such test procedure would be both impersonal and antisocial. The reader will gather that we are not referring to the testing of behaviour in the sense of Skinnerian terminal responses to a conditioning process masquerading as education.

No school, college or university which believed its aims to be educational—save perhaps a Benthamite panopticon—could be satisfied with its work if its students did not gain in personal stature and social awareness while passing through.

It has become customary to refer to this aspect of an educational institution's work as its 'hidden curriculum'. This is neither a useful term nor an accurate one. In most schools the hidden curriculum is blatant. We cannot hear what the school is saying because we are deafened by what it is.

We claim to have as our aim the encouragement of originality and creativity as well as the development of a critical faculty based on a sound understanding of logical thought and informed by a proper regard for evidence. We hope to inculcate self-respect as a precondition of respect for others. While hoping to avoid the pitfall of the 'soul of a prig housed in the body of a barbarian', we still hope to educate the whole man—or woman.

Yet all too often the message that is given loudly and clearly is that conformity is preferred to originality, creativity is suspected, critical faculties are limited by being banned in the thing that matters most to the student—the education he is receiving. If criticism of the institution is seen as disloyal and impertinent, appreciation is likely to be rare or insincere.

The NFER report *The Sixth Form and its Alternatives* investigates the attitude of differing kinds of school and college to the essentially trivial concern that plays so disproportionate a role in English education, namely uniform. All the comprehensives had school uniform and seven (out of fifteen in the sample) required their sixth-formers to wear it. Most of the schools reported that 'mild forms of (long hair on boys and jewellery and make up on girls) were permitted'.[25] 'School uniform was "compulsory" in all the grammar schools but in four (out of twelve) this rule did not apply to sixth-formers'.[26] But there was strong discouragement in the four of long hair styles and jewellery.

In sixth form colleges half allowed the students to dress as they pleased with a noteworthy lack of qualification by their principals.

In all the colleges of further education and tertiary colleges students were allowed to dress as they pleased. One is tempted to ask if the teaching profession has a sufficient sartorial reputation to lay down standards of fashion and hair-styling. Of course the matter has nothing to do with helping young people to dress appropriately. This can be done best by example. No college has any difficulty in getting young people to change for physical education or to wear overalls and safety glasses in workshops.

Where the insistence on uniform and approved hair styles is not mere habit on the part of the school, it is a deliberate 'put-down'. To force a young man or woman to dress as a boy or girl is an offence to their dignity. In the words of a grammar school pupil:

> Although it may just seem like sour grapes, I feel rather disillusioned with my sixth form course. One is led to believe that relations with staff will improve, one will instantly be treated as an adult and one will have ample time for private study, when in actual fact I found none of this was so. One is still restricted unnecessarily and expected to abide with petty rules.[27]

If the uniform and hair style obsession was merely an odd quirk of a system essentially open and liberal, it would not deserve the space we have given to it. Unfortunately it is not so. Too much of our education is concerned with packaging knowledge in a way which destroys the student's ability to relate things learned to his life. The petty restrictions reflect our fear of the young adult, so energetic, potent, and perceived as our rival. Schools can all too often praise banality of thought, conformity of attitude, and the second rate in the arts as these are safer. It is salutary to remember the number of brilliant men and women who have loathed school.

When we earnestly debate the curriculum we must remember that young people have to live in educational institutions for much of their time. If students feel that they are not respected and that their role is restricted to being a potential examination result, then all our curriculum planning will have been in vain.

Notes

1   Dean, J., and Weiner, G., *One Year Courses at 16 + : Six Case Studies and Some Tentative Conclusions,* (Slough, NFER, 1979), p.3. Reports on earlier research by NFER showed that a sample of 365 students following full-time GCE O-level courses in 1974—75 in a range of colleges and sixth forms attempted an average of 4.2 subjects but passed only 1.4

2   Peterson, A. D. C., *The Future of the Sixth Form* (London, Routledge and Kegan Paul, 1973) p.22.

3   Dean, J. and Weiner, G. *op.cit.,* p.155

4   Peterson, A. D. C., *The International Baccalaureate* (London, Harrap, 1972)

5   *Fifteen to Eighteen:* Report of the Central Advisory Council (Crowther Report) (London, HMSO, 1959)

6   Hargreaves, D., *Social Relations in the Secondary School* (London, Routledge and Kegan Paul, 1967), p.189

7   Lawton, D., *Social Change, Educational Theory and Curriculum Planning* (London, University of London Press, 1973), p.159

8   PSC stands for the Private Secretary's Certificate, a two-year secretarial course with a four GCE O-levels entry, a good course but unacceptable to higher education

9   Nill, C. and Pety, L., *Verzahnung von beruflicher und allgemeiner Bildung in der Kollegschule Nordrhein-Westfalen* (Berlin, Pädagogisches Zentrum, 1979)

10 Bloom, B. S., *The Taxonomy of Education Objectives,* (London, Longmans, 1956)

11   The BEC General Diploma was specifically designed to meet the
     criticisms outlined
12   *Proposals for a Certificate of Extended Education:* Report of the
     Study Group under the Chairmanship of Professor K. W. Keohane
     (London, HMSO, 1979), para.146
13   Dean, J., and Weiner, G. *op.cit.,* p.21
14   Keohane Report, *op.cit.* (note 12), para. 142
15   *ibid.,* para. 144
16   *ibid.,* para. 151
17   *ibid.,* para. 151
18   *Findings of the Committee on Technician Courses and Examinations:*
     Haslegrave Report (London, DES and NACEIC, 1969). This report
     was the origin of proposals to coordinate technician education
     through two national bodies such as BEC and TEC
19   Statistics on job-loss to Third World competition, from an Economic
     Intelligence Unit report, commissioned by the Foreign Office and
     published in *The Sunday Times,* 10 February 1980
20   T. H. Huxley extract quoted in Sagan, C., *The Dragons of Eden.*
     Speculations on the Evolution of Human Intelligence (London,
     Hodder and Stoughton, 1977) p.228
21   Toyne, P. (director) *Educational Credit Transfer Feasibility Study*
     (London, DES, Nov. 1979)
22   *ibid.* (shortened version), p.3
23   *ibid.* (shortened version), p.3
24   *ibid.* (shortened version), p.4
25   Dean, J., Bradley, K., Choppin, B., and Vincent, D., *The Sixth Form*
     and its Alternatives (Slough, NFER, 1979), p.54
26   *ibid.,* p.58
27   *ibid.,* p.169

5

STUDENT AFFAIRS: A COOPERATIVE APPROACH

A. B. Cotterell

The notion of student affairs is an American invention. Its rise to prominence in the United States corresponds with the phenomenal development of that country's economy and the equally amazing expansion of post-compulsory education underpinning such growth. In recent years the need for renewal has generated many new forms of adult learning—community colleges, universities without walls, competency-based programmes, to name but a few experimental approaches—and at the same time has drawn attention to the total development of students within all educational institutions. Whereas student development programmes have tended to run in parallel with formal instruction and be regarded as supplementary, there is now a considerable body of opinion advocating parity of esteem between class and out-of-class education so that college life can become a significant experience in itself. As one commentator sagely remarked:

> Reform of curriculum is not enough. Reform of the school is probably not enough. The issue is one of man's capacity for creating a culture, society, and technology that does not only feed him but keep him caring and belonging.[1]

It is implied that out-of-class educational experiences act as a catalyst for integrating the human personality and ensuring the triumph of humane learning. At the minimum they should preclude the graduate arsonist.

An imperative behind the student affairs movement is awareness of the increasing complexity of our time. Even in the 1960s nearly 50 per cent of the American college-age population was enrolled in high schools because of the increasing demand for skilled and specialised personnel. As in England and Wales, the staying-on rate has continued to rise since then. For these young adults—the 16 to 19 year-olds in British parlance—a number of needs have been identified by American student affairs organisers. They offer a useful starting-point for discussion of the tertiary college.

First, the student has to achieve competence, intellectually and physically. He needs confidence in his own ability to cope with the demands placed on him by a course of study. Secondly, the young adult has to learn how to manage his own emotions. Social abilities are not always well developed because adolescents lack experience in handling egalitarian relationships with their contemporaries apart from a situation in which they are invariably subordinate to adults. Without self-confidence and social skills there is little chance of satisfying the third perceived need, autonomy. As the individual approaches adulthood, increasing independence entails increasing responsibility for taking decisions, which progressively become more serious. Choice moves through friends and pastimes to studies and career, and will eventually encompass a marriage partner: decisions no human being can make for another. The fourth need is the establishing of an identity, that inner consistency which gives shape and meaning to the personality. To achieve this, the young adult must possess a modicum of wisdom and understand something of his physical needs, characteristics, and personal appearance, relating the newly acquired self-knowledge to the heightened interest between the sexes. Along with inner integration too should go a developing tolerance and respect for other people, whatever their abilities or disadvantages. Education ought to impart

> respect for the powers of thought concerning the human condition, man's plight and his social life . . . a sense of respect for the capacities and plight of man as a species, for his origins, for his potential, for his humanity.[2]

A final need of the young adult is purpose. Clarification of future aims including vocational and leisure-time plans should result in greater motivation. The desire for a closer contact with adult life is a distinct feature of the 16 to 19 year-old and teachers can play a vital role in helping students to select a sensible direction. Appreciation of such grown-up advice was expressed by a tertiary student in the NFER report, *The Sixth Form and its Alternatives,* who said:

> I find the small groups and close relationships with tutors helpful, as well as the fact that each group is under the care of a tutor who keeps a check on progress, even though students are encouraged to work independently without being told to work all the time. So although 'pastoral care' is given, and tutorial guidance is a strong feature of the college, students are treated as adults and are expected to organise their work of their own accord.[3]

Environmental Management

Though 1984 is nigh, the management of a college environment does not necessarily entail manipulation. The phrase is used here instead of atmosphere, ambience or ethos for the reason that it is not generally realised how important 'the feel' of an educational institution is to 16 to 19 year-olds and how easy it is to lose their approval. Environmental management consists in the active cooperation of all college members—teachers, non-teaching staff, and students—to organise resources so that students get the most out of their college experience. Managing a college environment does not mean controlling it. A principal cannot delegate such a task to one of his lieutenants. On the contrary, he would be advised to take a close interest in how the policies and decisions of the college management are apprehended by staff *and* students. This is perhaps the most crucial part of his duties. Understanding the strengths and limitations of his own character and knowledge is the starting point, not least because subordinates will take their cue from the principal's behaviour. With this self-knowledge in mind, he can inform himself about staff and student members of the college, constantly monitoring the interaction between these two key elements.

For students the tertiary college subsumes a vital phase of maturation. The 16 to 18 year divide is a difficult one to cross. It is the threshold of adulthood, especially since the lowering of the voting age from 21 years, and therefore the college environment has to cater for the developmental needs of students leaving adolescence. Neither the supermarket approach to learning, courses taken from the shelf with the minimum of staff contact, nor that of the claustrophobic corner shop, where a cross-examination is involved in any transaction, is likely to prove successful. College organisation has to suit both the self-reliant student and the least independent student as well as the numerous stages of maturity found between. In effect the college has to take seriously the student as an individual, whatever his needs, and through close liaison with parents and, if appropriate, employers assist him in the passage to citizenship. Study is not enough. 'Learning (in the widest sense of the word) and emotion, the cognitive and affective aspects of development, intellect and feelings', Mia Kellmer Pringle reminds us, 'are so closely interwoven and from so early an age as to be almost indivisible'.[4]

Environmental management, if properly conducted, leaves room for student affairs. The new experiences available in post-compulsory education do facilitate mental growth. Student opinion is quite pronounced on this point. An 18 year-old tertiary student left the NFER researchers in no doubt:

> On the whole I think that a college is much better than carrying on in a school. You are treated as an adult, not as a child. You learn and are expected to use your own initiative. A much greater understanding is gained of people and of the world. Much more general knowledge is gained not just about your career but about life as a whole. You learn to mix with people more than you would at school. You meet different people of varying backgrounds and altogether it is much more interesting.[5]

In large institutions, the sheer numbers, the proliferation of courses, the limited participation in extracurricular activities can sharply reduce the possibilities for developing relationships outside small, informal groups formed after chance encounters. Yet a conscious attempt to overcome the potential dangers of size can work, as the student quoted above demonstrates. Interestingly it is often thoughtful students themselves who initiate schemes to combat isolation and loneliness. At Richmond upon Thames College, the first tertiary leavers to have completed two-year courses there pinpointed the lack of adequate communal facilities as the institution's greatest weakness. An ex-President of the Students' Union said:

The best thing so far is the Common Room . . . It helped us a lot having a relatively new place. The students have been able to identify with it more than the old prefabricated hut image of the former Common Room. It helps having a decent office close by as well so that the Executive can actually come into some sort of contact with the students who use it. Of course there is still not enough room for getting together informally.

Another student, an ex-Vice-President, also singled out the improvement of the quality of daily life outside classes as the chief duty of a student organisation. She suggested that 'only through making things better for the mass of students will it be possible to get them more involved in college life'. What is being sought here is a purposeful relationship between formal learning and the student's personal growth. Both these young adults recognised that their contemporaries need practice in social skills and the exercise of responsibility. 'At least', commented an ex-Student Governor, 'we are positively encouraged to help ourselves. We have not got enough student activities going yet, nor have enough members of staff come forward to help different groups. Our communications are still poor. But the Principalship has let us run things for ourselves without interference, unlike some places nearby'. Cooperation may not always achieve the desired results as quickly as hoped, but the advantages of having common institutional goals cannot be gainsaid. Organisational arrangements which either inhibit exchange between individual students or tend not to foster emotional and social potential represent an unworthy diminution of student life. They fail to contribute to the task of training young adults for responsibility.

The Role of Student Organisations

Integral to environmental management is the formation of student organisations. Under further education regulations there is scope for setting up a students' union subject to the ratification of its constitution by the governing body of a college, and such annually elected organisations are familiar to the post-compulsory students outside of school and the sixth form college. The formal aims of the Students' Union in Richmond upon Thames College are not untypical. They are:

(1) To promote cooperation amongst its members for social, cultural and athletic activities.

(2) To provide a channel of communication between the students and the college authorities and external bodies and to represent its members' interests in all matters.

(3) To cooperate with the college authorities in setting and maintaining standards of student conduct.

Apart from providing the means for the democratic resolution of conflicts, such a student organisation acts as a channel for student aspirations as well as student creativity within the college environment. The extent of the impact of a students' union on a college depends on several factors. Obviously the attitude of the college authorities is relevant, as the ex-Student Governor has already observed. This attitude will also influence that of a Local Education Authority, which fixes the level of financial aid a students' union receives. Some institutions find their student organisations moribund because of lack of funds. Serious young adults are hardly tempted to devote time and energy to an organisation without the means of financing reasonable projects. In Richmond the level of support in 1980 was £4.50p per full-time student. The annual income of about £7000 allowed the Students' Union to finance extracurricular activities, run its communal facilities and participate in national student affairs. As the ex-Student Governor, who had personal experience in both sixth form and tertiary colleges, also cautioned:

> You have got to cater for minority interests in a large college. You cannot cater for the student body as a whole. You have got to realise that there are groups who want to do their thing, and just because they are in a minority, you cannot ignore them. This is why a students' union is so important. In a small college you may know who to approach for this, that, and the other, but in a large college like this there are so many people in so many different sections that we need a union with representatives of all these sections to be the centre, the focal point of student ideas and requests. It is the only way to find out what is really wanted.

This is the student organisation as repository of student views, the prime communication network outside the curriculum.

A severe constraint, however, on student organisation is the amount of time demanded from elected officers. Sabbatical presidents are no solution—one person cannot undertake all the jobs involved—and they are costly, besides in the context of the tertiary college being somewhat inappropriate. The effectiveness of a students' union for the 16 to 19 age group seems to depend on the availability of professional assistance. The informal approach of Youth and Community staff would appear the best answer to the problems of commitment and continuity.

The size of an institution may also be an important determinant of the extent to which students feel they play a significant role in its functioning. In the tertiary college, ideally with about 1250 full-time students, the decision-making machinery of the students' union may seem remote from the majority of students. Experience at Richmond upon Thames College shows that the strength of feeling among the student body about the remoteness of the Union Executive is inversely proportional to the efficiency of the Students' Union itself. Effective elected officers have taken an active part in the running of the college not only through the Students' Union but more as respected members of college committees. It is this linkage between student deliberation and staff deliberation which is the basis of environmental management.

Student Care and Discipline

The educational purpose of student organisations is the fostering of self-discipline. Autocratic discipline will not encourage self-control and the capacity to cooperate in the 16 to 19 year-old. The aim of environmental management in the tertiary college must be the creation of a young adult world, in which good student behaviour is inner-directed, the result of wishing to be treated as a grown-up. Some teachers find handling the transition between the unsettled 16 year-old and the more mature 18 year-old far from easy. Students do have problems making the adjustment to adulthood, but consistent and reasonable expectations on the part of staff are conducive to emphasising the value of internal controls. As one sixth-former complained in the NFER report:

> The least satisfactory part of my course has been over-rigid discipline. I feel sixth-formers should be allowed to spend free time as they wish and not be forced to remain in school. This would be more like college/university and would also fit better with the idea that sixth-formers are adults, not children being constantly watched.[6]

In contrast a tertiary respondent, who saw the need for a regulated pattern of behaviour, stated:

> In attending the college I have found it useful from a social point of view and educationally beneficial. I can only say that I have enjoyed every minute of college life and have found it much more conducive to work than school. The atmosphere is relaxed, yet enough discipline exists for the college to run smoothly.[7]

The young adult 'atmosphere' should embrace all courses and all students within a tertiary institution. It cannot be a privilege of A-level GCE students alone. The right to study in a mature way belongs to all students, given their differences at 16 years of age. For the working class the tertiary college ought to be a university experience.

The idea of the student contract is uncontaminated by discipline as punishment. Providing a tertiary college is timetabled on a modular basis, it is feasible for each student to have an individual timetable, specially devised to meet personal needs. This mutually agreed timetable at Richmond upon Thames College serves as a contract between the student and the college. It determines attendance and course work. Drawn up in consultation with the student and his parents by a Director (a member of staff responsible for students and courses), the timetable can only be altered by negotiation between the parties concerned. In order to ensure that a student fulfils his part of the contract—that is to say, that he attends regularly and completes work set by subject teachers—the Director receives information on progress via a pastoral tutor and details of absence via a weekly computer print-out. Failure to keep to the contract is investigated and its source analysed, with varying consequences: remedial help, a change of course, improved teaching arrangements, counselling, admonishment, a careers interview, a decision to seek employment. In each case the student is dealt with as an individual. The ultimate decision should not be seen as a disciplinary matter but rather the satisfactory resolution of a student's problem.

Success cannot be guaranteed by any system, for it will always be as good as the people who operate it, and doubtless there will exist forever the student bent on evading detection and beating the system, like a challenged child. Yet, in the words of a Richmond upon Thames College student, the open campus regime has a maturing influence on most 16 to 19 year-olds:

There are people who dodge lessons. I know several from my old school who are not working properly. Mind you, they were never very keen on studying there. But most of my friends really like the freedom in the college. You have work to do on your own, and it is your own business to get on and do it. That makes you organise your life. At my school private study hardly existed, and it took me some time to learn how to work on my own here. Teachers were very helpful and of course the study area in the library is excellent.

It would seem that this 17 year-old has acquired both competence and self-confidence. Students' views on free time for private study or for relaxation were found by the NFER report to be less dependent on the type of institution they attended than on the type of course they were following.[8] The tertiary college in this respect has to review its further education heritage. Over-teaching is good neither for the student nor the subject.

Counselling and Guidance Services

In 1974 the Comparative Research Unit of King's College, University of London, published the findings of a three-year inquiry into the educational and social implications of the expansion of upper-secondary education in England and four other countries. Entitled *Post-Compulsory Education: A New Analysis in Western Europe,* the report uncovered widespread dissatisfaction among the 16 to 19 age group over the quality and quantity of counselling and careers guidance then available in schools and colleges. Although English students felt that they had received more information, advice and guidance than their contemporaries in France, Italy, Sweden and the Federal Republic of Germany, they indicated strongly that counselling and guidance services were concerned much more with education than employment. Whereas 36 per cent of the English students in the sample said that they had received a lot of help about education, only 19 per cent could say the same about help over employment. In fact 27 per cent claimed to have had hardly any help over employment, and another 12 per cent no help at all.[9] Generally speaking the thrust of their criticism was against the assumptions of teachers, who placed over-emphasis on traditional fields of employment such as the Civil Service, the Services, and Banking. 'Instead, students asked for coverage of a wider and more imaginative range of opportunities, particularly in the field of employment, without the built-in assumption that students would pursue further full-time studies immediately... This suggests,' the researchers concluded, 'that in some cases a gulf or time-lag exists between students' perceptions and those of counselling and guidance staff, whose values and outlook are more traditional in nature.'[10]

Reflected in the students concern about the lack of first rate information on employment are two major changes at work in Britain. On one hand there is the 'new' population staying-on after the statutory school leaving age, and the correspondingly wider spread of ability and aspiration among 16 to 19 year-olds; on the other, we have the transformation of the economy since 1960. Teachers who have counselling responsibilities need to keep in touch with the current employment structure, its needs and its newly developing fields. Young adults are oriented towards work—the advent of youth unemployment has sharpened interest—so that to a greater extent than ever before students are seeking detailed and informed advice on career prospects, short- and medium-term.

In 1980 a questionnaire very similar to the one used by the Comparative Research Unit was completed by a number of students at Richmond upon Thames College. Since at its inception, counselling and guidance services were designed as an integral part of college organisation, and staffed accordingly, there seemed to be a reasonable chance of gauging student opinion about such aid. The results are set out in the following tables.

Students' assessment of the information or guidance provided in Richmond upon Thames College about employment, education and health

Amount	Employment (%)	Education (%)	Health (%)
A lot	8	40	0
Some	42	35	13
Hardly any	25	15	22
None at all	25	10	65

Students' assessment of the information available in the college according to future aspirations

Amount	Aspirations						
	Higher education (%)	Other full-time studies (%)	Employment with further training (%)	Employment without training (%)	Services	None of these	Do not know
Much more	28	5	21	3	—	—	—
A little more	12	—	3	5	—	—	3
Neither more nor less	8	3	3	3	—	3	—
A little less	—	—	—	—	—	—	—
Much less	—	—	—	—	—	—	—

Students' assessment of information and guidance on employment, education and health

Assessment	Employment (%)	Education (%)	Health (%)
Very helpful	13	35	3
Fairly helpful	37	40	12
Not really helpful	20	15	17
Not helpful at all	22	5	50
No reply	8	5	18

Health was added to the questionnaire because of the increasing numbers of students asking for medical advice. At the time of the sample an appointment for a college nurse had been approved but no one was in post. The counselling and guidance service comprised a college counsellor, a welfare officer, a first aid assistant, a college careers officer, and three careers officers and a receptionist seconded from the LEA Careers Service.

Significantly, the students' perceptions of the information and guidance available were not unlike the 1974 findings. Despite the relatively generous staffing of professional careers officers, less than 10 per cent of the students considered they received a lot of help about employment. In the no help at all category, the figures were even more startling: employment 25 per cent, education 10 per cent, and health 65 per cent.

How did this return happen? Some conclusions can be deduced from the comments made by students on the questionnaire. What immediately springs to attention is that employment advice was sought as much by students intending to go on to higher education as by those about to enter employment. When asked about the sort of information and guidance likely to be found most useful, such answers as these were given:

> About grants, lodgings for colleges, and the kind of job I could get after higher education.

> Areas of study suited to the chosen career and meeting people already at work.

> Information on what jobs are available after university.

. . . how A-levels, degrees and other qualifications relate to employment and which ones employers prefer.

Information at the beginning of courses on careers that the courses will lead to and the qualifications necessary for certain careers.

. . . polytechnics and universities and what careers are open to me.

Careers after university.

More information on employment—for the future.

I would like more information about a wider assortment of jobs.

Apart from details of courses at other colleges, it would also be beneficial to know what types of careers these would lead on to.

Graduate unemployment is obviously a factor here, but equally apparent is the insatiable appetite of students for up-to-date, realistic and detailed information on the whole range of postgraduate career opportunities. The 42 per cent of the sample who thought that they had received some help included many of the students going on to higher education. Their uncertainties over future employment relate to the widening range of alternatives as well as the need to keep options open for as long as possible in our rapidly changing world. Their dilemma is complicated by the lack of a national policy on continuing and recurrent education. Adaptability and flexibility are being called for at all levels of employment, as altering circumstances require constantly the renewal of knowledge. There is no sense in which any course of higher education can now be looked upon as a complete preparation for work.

The need to be adaptable and flexible in our concepts of education and training is paramount. Both teachers and students have to be aware of the consequences of technological change. In terms of counselling and guidance it means that a tertiary college must establish a dual system. Apart from the day-to-day problems dealt with by a pastoral tutor, students should have the right of access to trained counselling and guidance staff on a confidential basis. Unless such detached and anonymous help is available in a tertiary college, whatever the size of its student body, there is a real danger of alienation among the 16 to 19 age group. The institution, by definition, embraces locally the entire range of courses available to young adults and therefore must contain within itself a mechanism for reassessment of course or career choice which does not prejudice the status of students. Such internal flexibility is difficult to attain, not least because the system of early specialisation in the secondary schools often pre-empts a change of direction. Students can discover at 16-plus that they do not possess the qualifications needed for their particular choice of job or course.

Liaison between compulsory and post-compulsory institutions is essential. The college careers officer and college counsellor have a vital function in the interchange of information and advice between a tertiary college and its feeder schools. While personal details may be passed on to the college—in some Local Education Authorities this is normal practice—there is a possibility that sensitive information will not be communicated. Informal contact between those charged with pastoral care in schools and the college counselling and guidance staff would appear most desirable. There is a body of opinion which strongly condemns the transfer of records, arguing for a fresh start for each student in post-compulsory education. Certainly the assessment of handicap or disadvantage can in itself cause problems. 'There are dangers of "giving a dog a bad name" and of making intimate and detailed information about personal family problems available to a considerable number of people,' Sir Alec Clegg has pointed out, 'but the real danger of an "at risk" register is that teachers who handle children might become obsessed by their search for problems and their expectation of them. The effect of this could be that problems would be seen where they are not important or that they were exaggerated far beyond their educational significance.'[11]

Given the importance that students clearly attached to an individual approach, the duties of counselling and guidance staff might be set out as follows:

(i) *Pre-entry.* Liaison with secondary schools so as to exchange information particularly about changes in college courses, career opportunities, curriculum, examinations, transfer procedures; to participate in careers conventions and parents evenings at schools; to interview potential students where their choice of course or career seems uncertain.

(ii) *College progress.* In association with other staff—course directors and personal tutors—the encouragement of students to review their progress in the light of up-to-date information on opportunities in employment, further and higher education; the provision of a personal advisory service for students, whether referred by staff or by themselves; the monitoring of college courses as regards their value to students and employers.

(iii) *Placement.* The placement of students in further or higher education institutions or into work; the organisation of a careers information service, including a library, talks by visiting speakers concerning employment and education, visits to firms and colleges, work experience; the arrangement of interviews for students leaving the college before the completion of a course; the gathering of statistics on placement.

The success of these activities depends to a great extent on the knowledge and experience of the staff involved and the degree to which they coordinate their efforts. Counselling and guidance services must equally relate to the comprehensive aims of the tertiary college. Students need to be assured that the advice they receive is unbiased and sensible, but even more they need to be confident that no reasonable possibility within education or employment has been closed down to them.

Student Progress

The final year of compulsory education should include some experience in private study in order that the transition to college does not prove traumatic. Just as the need for students intending to go on to higher education to acquire the necessary study skills in the sixth form has been recognised, so it is becoming apparent that in a lesser but no means unimportant way the secondary school pupil requires preparation for post-compulsory study. The ability to study on one's own and to assume responsibility for one's own work schedule is the basis of academic progress. Self-directed learning may well be the pattern of most adult education in the future, when the renewal of knowledge could be the sole method of personal survival as an employee, but even now the advantages of independent private study are becoming understood.

Adjustment to the demands of post-O-level GCE courses is not easily accomplished. The NFER report found that students in all educational institutions encountered some difficulty. Students also

noted the general absence of guidance and tuition given to them in
making the changeover from a broad and general course of O-levels
to a more analytical and specialised one of A-levels. One focused
the issue precisely:

> For at least some of the earlier part of the course, it would be better,
> instead of giving students 'study periods' to give classes on 'how to
> study'. This is done in some American universities and the results are
> supposed to be encouraging.[12]

Advice given by a tutor should of course encompass study skills,
but in a tertiary college the library ought to act as a learning environment too. It should house a learning resource and study centre, to which students can repair for assistance—whether for
research skills, help with the organisation of information, or
specific learning problems. One student, for instance, might seek
instruction in fast reading, another in spelling. What is crucial,
however, is that such a back-up service exists and is widely publi-
cised. As a student at Richmond upon Thames College commented:

> The fact that assistance is available is not enough. There should be
> plenty of publicity about counselling and guidance. Students have to
> be encouraged much more to think about and use the facilities on of-
> fer.

Under further education regulations students are not required to
register every morning and are able to come and go as timetabled.
For this reason a large and well-run library plays an integral part in
the learning process of a tertiary college. Its work tables are the
laboratory for student experiments in independent study.

Student progress is the purpose of student affairs. For the tertiary college this means treating its 16 to 19-year-olds as adults and
allowing them to come to terms with those internal and external
factors which must determine course and career choice. Interests,
abilities and attainments have to be balanced against the requirements of course and job, as well as future prospects and life-
style. In the words of one mature 18 year-old at Richmond upon
Thames College:

> I think staff ought to know the difference between students who need
> to be treated more as if they have just come out of school, because
> they are not used to being in a college yet, from students who don't.
> There is a terrific difference between a young 16 year-old and an old 17
> year-old. The atmosphere in the college would be impossible if we

were not allowed to grow up freely. Providing things are explained to them, most of the students behave responsibly anyway. Why shouldn't they?

Perhaps the young man has divined one of the strengths of the tertiary college, its assumption of maturity. Evidence in the NFER report would suggest that the traditional sixth form is not seen as providing an equivalent experience for most of its members. The report concludes that the tertiary college of the future

> ...does not represent an FE takeover, as some critics of the tertiary system would seem to suggest, but a synthesis of the best of both systems incorporating the further education sector's flexibility, responsiveness to industry, technical and vocational experience and the secondary sector's experience in academic teaching and emphasis on pastoral care.[13]

Notes

1 Bruner, J. S., 'The Process of Education Revisited', *Phi Delta Kappan,* (Sep. 1971), 18 – 21, quoted in Miller, T. K. and Prince, J. S., *The Future of Students Affairs. A Guide to Student Development for Tomorrow's Higher Education* (San Francisco, Jossey-Bass, 1976), pp. 2 – 3

2 Bruner, J. S. *et al., Studies in Cognitive Growth* (New York, Wiley 1966), Chap. 2

3 Dean, J., Bradley, K., Choppin, B., and Vincent, D., *The Sixth Form and its Alternatives* (Slough, NFER, 1979), p.185

4 Pringle, M. K., *The Needs of Children* (London, Hutchinson, 1975), p.33

5 Dean, J.,*et al., op.cit.* p.184

6 *Ibid,* p.163

7 *Ibid,* p.184

8 *Ibid,* pp.166 – 8

9 King, E. J., Moor, C. H., and Mundy, J. A., *Post-Compulsory Education: A New Analysis in Western Europe,* London and Beverly Hills, Sage, pp.347 – 8, 1974

10 *Ibid,* p.361

11 Clegg, A., *Recipe for Failure* (London, National Children's Home, 1972), p.66 (the 1972 Convocation Lecture of the National Children's Home, London).

12 Dean, J., *et al., op.cit.,* pp.270 – 1

13 *Ibid.,* p.326

6

ACCOUNTABILITY VERSUS AUTONOMY

E. W. Heley

That educational institutions should be accountable is denied by no one. That they should have some measure of autonomy is denied by few. The problem is therefore one of definition. The prevailing tendency, or perhaps the tendency of those in society who prevail, is towards a greater degree of accountability and less of autonomy. Schools and colleges must take some share of the blame for the decline in economic performance of the country. This was admitted in Essay 2. The dashing of the high and unrealistic expectations entertained after the Second World War of the benefits of an extension of educational opportunity has now led to equally unrealistic criticisms of the system and, since English schools and their teachers traditionally enjoyed an autonomy which was unusually liberal, to increasing demands for greater control over the curriculum and school organisation.

The ball was set rolling by the Prime Minister James Callaghan in October 1976, who spoke to a departmental brief that was leaked to the press. Of the four topics that interested Mr Callaghan the last—the general problem of 16 to 19 year-olds who have no prospect of going on to higher education—is particularly relevant to this book. The basic premisé of the speech was that teacher autonomy had been allowed to go on too long without scrutiny by those groups in society who had a right to be concerned:

parents, teachers, learned and professional bodies; representatives of higher education and both sides of industry together with the government, all have an important part to play in formulating and expressing the purposes of education and the standard that we need.[1]

It will be noted that in this lengthy list of concerned interested parties young people themselves were not thought worthy of inclusion. It is to be hoped that those teachers who have long resisted the notion that students should have some say in their own education may now come to see their students as allies in repelling the narrower forms of concern being expressed. For the education system is under attack and its response is uncertain and unduly defensive. Supposedly it has been found wanting and responsible for current ills ranging from football hooliganism to a shortfall in technologists. It is even incompatibly castigated for creating mindless pop-crazed hedonists or intellectual permissive radicals dedicated to the overthrow of civilisation as we know it. It has simultaneously, it seems, spawned a generation which cannot think for itself and one that shows a disturbing lack of deference to authority. Despite an increasing share of the GNP and the extension of the period of schooling standards are said to have declined. If it is suggested that this is not the case; the number of young people with GCE A-level qualifications can be shown to have risen and the sales of the quality press has risen with it; then the argument shifts to concern that standards are clearly not high enough to meet present needs. This attitude is a common one among those who view the past in a more roseate hue than we do. Once apparently schools produced young people who could all read and write and do long division by the age of 14 and did it much more cheaply than schools do now. As Barry MacDonald has written:

> ...the concept of 'standards' as a distillation of the past functions as a powerful deterrent to variety and development in schools. By such standards schools will always be seen to be doing a poorer job than they used to. Thus, it could be said, facetiously, that only illiteracy prevents more people from writing to the press to complain about the decline in reading. Thus too, we might understand why, when all but one of a number of reading surveys suggest the maintenance or improvement of attainment, that one exception appears to be more credible to the interested public than the sum of the others.[2]

The simplistic 'more has meant worse', 'the schools are failing the nation', and so on, has unfortunately considerable emotional appeal to a people simultaneously experiencing worsening economic conditions and future shock. It also confers advantage upon politicians willing to abandon intellectual scruples in the handling of evidence and moderation in the use of language. The habit of judging present-day educational standards by those of the past fails to notice that as society changes so does the concept of useful knowledge. It is not surprising that there has been less emphasis in our primary schools on 'tables' and mental arithmetic, for in the age of decimal money, metric units of weight, length and volume, computerised cash registers and ubiquitous pocket calculators arithmetic drills of the old elementary school type lose much of their cogency. Our children have more pressing concerns than the antics of idiots who run taps into baths with the plug out. Indeed a case could be made that far from curriculum innovation having gone mad, far too much of what is taught in schools comes from the lumber room—romantic Geography, irrelevant Anglo-centred History, French (why not Arabic or Mandarin Chinese?) agreed syllabuses of Religion, (agreed thirty years ago), 19th century science, 'Woodwork', ... English education has never been instrumental but has inherited from the education of an élite the notion of the development of the whole man. While the majority of us have to earn our living, that is not the whole of life. It would be retrograde to respond to the present economic climate by sacrificing the wider purposes of education. The autonomy of the teacher gives some hope of protecting innovation, response to student needs and eccentricity even, from the sterility of national standards. The education service, its constituent parts and the individual teacher must be analogous to the hospital service and individual doctors and nurses, never to the accountability of the branch and its staff to the head office of a firm. For while a branch manager may have some conscience in his dealings with his customers, who may in any case be protected from exploitation by consumer legislation or the law of contract, he will see his main function as dedication to the firm's aims and objectives. If he does not, he is unlikely long to remain branch manager. The headteacher or college principal cannot have such a simple model of accountability. If accountability is the duty to render account of work performed to a body that has authority to modify that performance by the use of sanction and reward, then the school or college would be responsive only to the Local Education Authority. Though this is a common enough view, teachers as professionals are accountable also to their professional ethic for the discharge of their responsibility to the student. If we could assume a universally benevolent, liberal and understanding LEA, no conflict would arise. Unfortunately, in the real world, the school or college finds itself beset by irreconcilable demands from politicians both national and local, employers and their organisations, parents, students themselves, pressure groups of all kinds, and a resolution can only be found in asserting as paramount the needs of the student.

The Problem

> Accountability or answerability relies on the assumption that public institutions and those who work in them should respond to community and social prescriptions. The underlying premise is collectivist. Institutional or professional autonomy . . . responds instead to individualist, or atomistic, assumptions which would confer initiative and freedom on the smallest units, preferably individual people.[3] .

Here Professor Kogan summarises the dichotomy between accountability and autonomy in education. Readers may note with surprise that those most vociferous in demanding the subservience of the state system of education to their perception of national needs would philosophically reject the collectivist implication of their position; and conversely the demand for teacher autonomy, an individualist concept, comes most stridently from those whose outlook is collectivist.

> It is agreed that English schools are protected from the centralised direction and uniform curricula of continental countries because of the autonomy granted to head teachers . . . But Ellis and the school came to grief because this theory does not accord with the practice. Power is granted to heads only so long as they exercise it in accordance with the wishes of the political masters.[4]

Thus wrote the suspended teachers of William Tyndale Junior School who had asserted autonomy unacceptable to the ILEA. It may be that the reversal in attitudes can be explained in the case of the individualists demanding accountability by their ambivalence towards state education. Many have been educated in the private sector. In the group, typified by the William Tyndale affair, the demand for autonomy is made in order to protect its view of the educational process from a hostile world.

The tension between autonomy and accountability cannot be resolved in an either/or way. It is an inherent and useful dialectic. Professor Kogan in the lecture referred to earlier makes a distinction between the autonomy of the individual teacher and what he calls the 'prime institution'. The teacher's autonomy will always be within broad prescriptive limits since he works within a social organisation (school or college) which for Professor Kogan is the autonomous unit in education. This definition of prime institution is:

> that role or collection of roles that has sufficient authority in terms of resources, legitimacy, public acceptance . . . to perform the core activities without recourse to the total system except for the most general prescriptions.[5]

Within this definition both primary and secondary schools are prime institutions. In effect the conflict between accountability and autonomy is fought out—or if this term is too belligerent a metaphor—resolved between the school and its controlling authorities. For the college of further education, as well as the tertiary college, the notion of the college as a whole as a prime institution is difficult to sustain except in a loose quasi-federal sense. Its complex internal organisation, its range of courses, its diversity of experience and qualifications of staff make a single monolithic interface with the outside unrealistic. Yet the Local Education Authority will be unwilling to treat a tertiary college as a confederation. It will expect the principal to take responsibility for all internal decision-making, even let it be noted when it has presented him with a policy-making academic board. The resolution of this dilemma is the development of a system of *internal* accountability. The autonomy of departments and sections must be limited. This can be achieved by organisational and management techniques expressed in a matrix system, outlined in Essay 5. It should be reinforced by demanding of the staff compliance with the highest professional standards both in and out of the classroom. A high degree of staff involvement in decision-making is a necessary corollary. We cannot expect staff to be professional giants in relation to students and pygmies in relation to the college hierarchy.

The tertiary college has to an extraordinary degree to be aware of the many strands of the current debate. It is legally a further education institution subject to a set of regulations which were drawn up for a different age and for a different kind of college. It is controlled by a Local Education Authority which decides on its size, resources, and place in the local education system. It has the vulnerability to criticism of a monopoly. It has to recognise the legitimate concern of parents. It has to maintain the confidence of local employers. Much of its work is subjected to external monitoring by examining bodies. Its HMIs come in pairs since it is both a vocational institution and a school. Its staff have different traditions of autonomy and accountability and have different attitudes to conditions of service. It has a large staff component who are not teachers: clerks, typists, technicians, reprographic operators, welfare workers, caretakers, groundsmen, cleaners, dinner-ladies, porters, secretaries; each group with its own hierarchies and priorities, some of which are not as can usually be assumed for the majority of teachers, primarily concerned with the well-being of the student.

The tertiary college recognises its salience in the accountability debate as it affects the provision for the 16 to 19 age group. The varied institutional arrangements—school, sixth form college, sixth form centre, consortia and tertiary colleges—operating under two entirely different sets of regulations neither of which serves its purpose in modern conditions have sharpened interest in this part of post-compulsory education.

At the time of writing a DES committee under the chairmanship of Mr Neil Macfarlane, Minister of State is reviewing the education of the 16 to 19 age group and is receiving evidence. The local authority associations have submitted a paper which makes demands for wider powers in this field than ever before.[6] They claim for themselves a more interventionist role in the education service. They say that the division of powers between LEAs, governing bodies and academic boards handicaps the effective management of institutions and any attempt to ensure the rational distribution and coordination of 16 to 19 education. They believe that governors and staff should be accountable to the LEA for the use of resources since, they suggest, there is disturbing evidence of bad management. They believe that they and not the Departmentof Education and Science should approve articles of government and lay down the role of governors—presumably a less powerful one in relation to the LEA—but a more interventionist one within the college. The DES has already made claims for a more indicative role in curriculum planning with HMI playing a more active part than at any time since 'payment by results' was abandoned.

It is clear that the education service is to be made more accountable, which is overdue and in many ways a welcome development. It would be a pity, however, if the demand for greater accountability is to be justified by assertions of bad practices. Accountability is desirable for its own sake in a free society. Professionals must be open to criticism and should welcome informed concern. The LEAs will hardly gain the cooperation they need if their stance is punitive and their aim is to intervene in a more detailed way than general prescription and a close monitoring of adherence to the prescription. The attitude of the National Association of Teachers in Further and Higher Education may be crucial. This most powerful of teacher unions has won for its members conditions of service that are variously viewed by school teachers as bordering on the unprofessional or alternatively with undisguised envy. NATFHE may regard the assertion of more extensive powers by LEAs as a threat to positions hardly won. The stage may be set for a controversy in which the landscape of educational administration will be changed in unexpected ways. Whereas the aim to assert the accountability of teachers and the institutions in which they work is legitimate, the impulse to regulate and control the day-to-day work of the teacher and to limit the exercise of professional discretion is not. If it is suggested that professional autonomy was expressed in practice as academic licence, we must beware that accountability does not in its turn become a recipe for direction, rigidity and reaction.

Auditing a College for Effective Performance

David Moore, the principal of Nelson and Colne Tertiary College has suggested a five-point scheme for auditing the performance of a college.[7] Accountability can only be realistic if there are agreed criteria for testing performance. Moore's points may be summarised as follows: First, the college should after the fullest consultation with its clientele, staff, and with the agreement of the authority publicly declare its aims and objectives. It is only against an objective that performance can be measured both as a college and internally by staff familiarity with and adherence to the objectives. Secondly, there should be an effective communications system for both staff and students. Thirdly, the college should have a reasonably sophisticated system of staff induction, development and training. Fourthly, the college should have established an individual student guidance system which functions outside the formal administrative structure. Last, because all its students are volunteers the college will demonstrate a positive approach to its community, responding to the needs of both majority and minority interests. This will involve committed and regular communication with all types of individuals and groups.

These five points are not exhaustive but they indicate that accountability concerns more than not exceeding the budget and keeping the young from being a nuisance. It is clear that many colleges would fail Moore's 'examination questions'. The reader might care to test them against either his local college of further education or the sixth form of a local school. Far from the objectives being clear and public, the usual stance of both is one of mystification and professional secrecy. If Aristotle thought the unexamined life was not worth living, it appears that many of our colleges and schools are in that position. The effective communication system is a rarity: the larger the organisation, the more it is needed and the less frequently it is found. Moore's own college, let us add, is a model in this respect. A centrally compiled newsletter regularly gives full information in classified form.

Yet new staff in institutions are often thrown into the classroom without help or guidance. They are expected to pick up information on how the college or school operates by sitting next to Nellie. Their careers seem to be at the mercy of mere chance as there is little or no planned development either in terms of qualifications or varied experience. Good staff are frustrated by this aimlessness; bad staff are not encouraged or helped to improve performance. While lip-service is paid to the need for people of all kinds to retrain and keep up-to-date, in-service training of teachers has been a casualty of economy. The James Report gathers dust in a ministerial pigeon-hole.[8]

Student guidance as Moore rightly suggests cannot be left as a 'form master' extra duty. Young people should have recourse to a sophisticated professional and disinterested agency within the college. Richmond upon Thames College has a professional group comprising a trained counsellor, welfare officer, nurse, careers tutor, seconded careers officers from the borough careers service, a student warden, and assistant student warden (both trained youth workers). These, as suggested, operate outside the pastoral care system of the divisions (departments), though they provide support to it. The staff in the group are answerable directly to the assistant principal responsible for student care and discipline.

The responsiveness of a tertiary college to the community it serves must be its most characteristic feature. For Nelson and Colne with its large adult education component and regional cultural centre, a stately home for the arts and crafts, this response will take a different form from Richmond upon Thames where the presence of a separate adult education college makes the tertiary college response to feeder schools and employers the two most important external relationships. There are no prescriptions other than the need to connect.

Moore's five points may not appear to be in the mainstream of concern about accountability but they are important for the light they shed on autonomy. A college can be accountable only for what it is responsible. A member of staff can be internally accountable only if he is free to make decisions within his job specification. Autonomy is a prior condition of accountability. For example, it is unbelievable but true that in some benighted areas of the country until recently headteachers were excluded from staff appointments. In no sense of natural justice should a head-teacher be held accountable for the performance of staff imposed upon him. The five points are all within the power of the college to set its own standards and therefore to be held accountable for meeting these.

The discussion on accountability has so far been limited to two levels, the institution and the teacher. There is a third level, the Local Education Authority itself. If the institutions are accountable to the LEA, to whom is the LEA in its turn accountable? *Quis custodiet ipsos custodes?* The easy answer is that the elected representatives are answerable to the electorate itself. Unfortunately the electorate is a heterogeneous body most of whose members are not parents with children. The electorate responds every few years to topical issues and national mood. Redress of educational grievance should not await such infrequent and uncertain arbitrage. The Education Committee should see itself answerable to parents for the education of their children. Even under Baines' corporate style management the Education Committee still has a wide measure of autonomy and is served by officers who retain considerable powers of discretion. If these are not used to defend and promote the education service it is difficult to see why these privileges should be retained.

The Education Committee of the London Borough of Richmond upon Thames publishes in detail the examination results of all its secondary schools as well as its tertiary college. This exercise in public accountability has like all such ventures been fraught with peril. Just as there are said to be lies, damned lies, and statistics, there are of properly compiled statistics, lying interpretations, damned lying interpretations, and the popular press. The Chairman of Richmond's Education Committee wrote to remonstrate at the way in which the borough's honest and detailed publication of results had been presented in two local newspapers. The first letter was to a newspaper which served in the main a nearby area in which the selection issue was still being fought bitterly. The alleged 'shocking results' were to be seen as an awful warning of what happens in areas that reorganise comprehensively. The second letter was to a newspaper whose circulation area is almost exactly the London Borough of Richmond upon Thames and is therefore more closely argued.[9]

(i)   *Chairman's letter to the Editor of the* Surrey Comet

The Editor
The Surrey Comet
20 Church Street
Kingston upon Thames, Surrey   5th November 1979

Dear Sir,
I was extremely sorry that you chose to treat—quite unjustifiably in my view—the publication of the examination results of our secondary schools in such an alarmist and misleading way. How a fractional—1.4%—fall in the number of GCE passes gained this year (2436 against

2471), a rise of no less than 17% in the number of GCE grade 'A', and a 4.9% increase in CSE passes, qualifies for banner headlines as a shocker I cannot begin to imagine. Taking CSE grade 1s as equivalent to a GCE pass our current level of GCE passes was exactly the same as last year.

I hope that in future the openness and care with which the borough treats its examination results will be repaid with the more understanding and responsible approach this important subject deserves.

Yours faithfully,

J. F. Lambeth
Chairman, Education Committee

(ii) *Chairman's letter to the Editor of the* Richmond and Twickenham Times

The Editor
Richmond and Twickenham Times
14 King Street
Richmond, Surrey   5th November 1979

Dear Sir,

I should like to comment briefly on the prominence you gave to the 'pass rate' and the league table in your reporting last week of our secondary schools' examination results.

In a selective system where pupils capable of taking the GCE examination are concentrated in grammar schools it is possible to use the pass rate as a measure of the effectiveness of the teaching of a school from one year to another and against another similar school's level of performance. In a comprehensive system, however, where the distribution of the most academically able pupils may be spread unevenly and differently from year to year, it is obviously dangerously mistaken to try to compare the effectiveness in examination performance of one school with another, unless we are sure that both are starting off with the same mix of ability and the same approach to entering pupils for public examinations. As far as the latter is concerned, comprehensive schools make very considerable attempts to include in external examination courses as many pupils as possible who will benefit from them, but who might not succeed in the end. It is obvious that the school which adopts the more generous approach stands a greater risk of spoiling its pass rate than the one which is not prepared to take the same chance with its borderline pupils.

Because of the discontinuance of testing with the introduction of comprehensive education, we do not know what distribution of ability took place in our secondary schools' entries five years ago. For this reason any idea of concluding from this year's results that one school is in any sense 'better' than another to the extent of arranging it in a list, whatever kind this may be, is not only futile but hurtful and unfair to those who must occupy the lower rungs. Last year we reintroduced standardised testing in the final year of all our primary schools so that the secondary schools would have an objective measure of the academic potential of their intake this year. Such tests must be used with caution, particularly where the individual child is concerned (they cannot, for example, take individual motivation into account), but they are a reasonably reliable guide for an overall comparison of the academic potential of one school's intake with another's, and it will be possible from the mid-80s for schools to set this information against public examination results to confirm that they are succeeding.

For there is no doubt that our secondary schools are continuing to achieve success in public examinations. That there are individual ups and downs among schools for the reasons I have explained reflects no discredit on the education offered in any school. What is important, and is an achievement in which our teachers may justly take pride, is that the combined results for all schools shows a success rate which compares well with national expectations.

As you say, parents have a right to know about a school's examination results. This borough was the first education authority in the country to publish this kind of information in useful detail. But schools and their pupils and parents also have a right to be free from the artificial competitive pressures created by league tables and the thoroughly bad practice which they can give rise to—heaping unnecessary O-levels on the most able and removing borderline pupils from examination classes merely to improve a school's reported standing in relation to others.

All detailed statistical information lends itself to a wide range of interpretations according to which isolated factor it is decided to highlight. Examination results are no exception. It is impossible to construct a single table which will give adequate expression to all the varying factors which go into examination results, let alone, in one list, to do justice to the numerous educational qualities which a comprehensive school must, as its name reminds us, embrace.

I hope, therefore, that when next year's results are before us, newspaper reporting will show a fuller understanding of the highly relative nature of published examination successes and reflect more accurately the place of examinations in the education system as a whole.

Yours faithfully,

J. F. Lambeth
Chairman, Education Committee

The points made by Lambeth about the secondary results also apply to those of the tertiary college. The more liberal its approach to examination entry, the less well the college comes out of crude comparisons with élitist sixth forms. A reputation as a 'good school' can be won spuriously by a school willing to dismiss its problem-students to be dealt with by open-access institutions or even ultimately by the forces of law and order. This problem is merely a clash between a version of accountability, a dressed-up shop window on one hand, and a genuine professional responsibility to the individual student on the other. The issue is particularly relevant to relations with employers. The further education system offers to industry and commerce a cost-effective and efficient training and educational programme. It gives the customer what he wants. The customer is in this case the employer and his agent the training officer of the firm. The college must be accountable to the employer for the quality of the course given to the employees. The judge of quality is however the firm and not the apprentice. A fundamental and almost unresolvable problem arises from the teacher's professional responsibility to the student. A firm may set limits to the development of the employee. The author remembers a training officer resisting the transfer of a successful one year Certificate of Office Studies student to an Ordinary National Certificate in Business Studies course on the grounds that the firm had no call for such well-educated labour and the lad would leave the firm and the cost of his training would be lost. No genuine teacher could accept such a proposition for a moment. Nor should he. Society is enriched by having well educated and trained people. It is made poorer by unrealised potential. The training officer's objections were not, in the long run, good for the firm either: under-achieving employees become bored and in some industries dangerous to themselves and others—they usually leave anyway. If the college in order to retain the goodwill of firms in its area becomes too complaisant, it runs the risk of treating the students as raw material for industrial processing. A relevant comment from an HMI report on a further education college was:

> The college ought to adopt a rather firmer attitude on educational matters and become a little more independent in this respect. It could do more to persuade good firms to be better and poorer firms to improve in their educational thinking.[10]

In short, the customer is not always right.

The tertiary college and the 11 to 16 schools bring into sharp focus the institutional autonomy claimed by schools and colleges. The relationship between the sixth form and the lower school is largely unexamined. The curriculum is regarded as a continuum, 11 to 18. The social mores and rituals are also thought of in unified terms, though this has tended to be a more dubious proposition in the last few years. The college of further education does not concern itself with organisational patterns nor the curricula of schools in its area. The usual stance is competitive. It stresses its differences from rather than its similarities to schools. This may be expressed in sixth form education by using different GCE Examining Boards. The Associated Examining Board with its practical bias and independence of university influence has a loyal customer in the further education sector. The associative life of the college is stressed in contrast to the community of the school. The college of further education knows that its real attraction to young people is precisely that it is not a school.

The wastefulness of this competition, the distortion of the purposes of education, the absurdity of it even, should be obvious. In areas where the statutary schooling period is organised in secondary schools and post-16 education in tertiary colleges, autonomy jealously defended as a way of resisting competitors becomes unnecessary and can be seen as a sacrifice of the best interests of the young.

One of the fears expressed about tertiary colleges is that they will become 'big brother' dictating the curricula to 11 to 16 schools. The unfortunate practice of calling them 'feeder schools', suggesting that they exist merely to provide students for the college, is likely to fuel the suspicion. The reverse is as likely to be true. The autonomy of the secondary school will impose on the college the need to provide end-on courses without consideration of cost-effectiveness or needs at sixth form level. There are teachers with sixth form experience in 11 to 16 schools now, but as time goes by the 11 to 16 sector will develop its own corps of teachers who will not have to the same degree a sensitivity to the requirements of the 16 – 18 stage. Here we have a clash of autonomy. There is a need for some pooling of sovereignty. The role of educational advisers in obtaining this can be decisive. They provide the honest brokers and impartial chairing of curriculum panels which is essential if the equality of all parties to the discussion is to be maintained. The location of meetings may be significant. Even if the tertiary college is central, meeting at a teachers' centre or in rotation at the schools, may be more effective. In Richmond, panels comprising joint meetings of subject staff and careers teachers are most successful. Since agreement at these levels need the approval of headteachers if they are to be translated into action, the principal of the college must play a full part in the deliberation of secondary heads. The process outlined is a two-way one. The college should be influenced in its choice of options and modes of learning by those adopted in the schools. An interchange of staff should become a normal part of the system. If regulations and Burnham make this difficult local authorities should buy a Nelson-style telescope. Informal meetings of teachers in the same disciplines, the frequent visits of senior staff of the college to schools and vice versa make for the development of understanding.

The disadvantages of the break at 16 are often alluded to. One of the many advantages is that in tertiary areas the schools become aware of the full implications of vocational education. The schools appreciate the need for subject continuity; German GCE A-level builds on German GCE O-level; but they are less aware of the need for care in the preparation of pupils for vocational courses. Examination options are usually chosen in the third year and the college must help schools to make pupils, parents and staff realise the critical nature of choice for future career opportunities. It would be fair to say that children in areas with tertiary colleges are served better in this respect than in those with 11 to 18 schools, because the Engineering, Construction, Business Studies and other vocational departmental heads are welcome visitors to the 11 to 16 schools and discuss their programmes with staff and pupils in an informal way. In 11 to 18 schools such help is seldom sought from the local college of further education and the advice given to young people is therefore too school-bound and subject-oriented.

The autonomy of the 11 to 16 school in its non-instrumental education is so far as the college is concerned as complete as the college claims for its own. Diversity in the 11 to 16 schools in extracurricular activities, in subject strengths, in general attitudes, adds to the colour and interest of the college experience. In Richmond the rugby players seem to come from one school, the actors from another.

The title of the chapter postulated a conflict between autonomy and accountability. It has been suggested that accountability cannot be a simple line-management model. Education is not a government agency but a service to society in which there are a multiplicity of functional relationships and responsibilities. The urge to make the service accountable in the production mode by testing and the imposition of standards ignores at least half of educational experience—some would say the better half. The process of education is more important than the end result. In education one travels hopefully. In a full life there is no arrival, for arrivals are like through stations, merely new points of departure. We can and should monitor the process, and consider what happens to students in the system:

> It involves asking how schools set about helping their pupils to realise their intellectual potential, develop their personal interests and become useful members of society. It calls for a discussion of current practice and possibly for some negotiation between teachers and parents about its acceptability and effectiveness. The aim behind the approach is educative or ameliorative. The emphasis is in credibility and accessibility. Commonly it involves a shift towards greater openness of information. It shares the relativity of any transaction between professional and client.[11]

Again we are driven back to the central relationship in education, that between the teachers and the taught. If this is felt to be right by both parties, then, as J. M. Barrie's Maggie in *What Every Woman Knows* said of charm, 'If you have it, you don't need to have anything else; if you don't have it, it doesn't much matter what else you have'. The system must be accountable to the student, who must have the right or redress not only in matters of discipline and welfare but in what teachers are often reluctant to concede—academic short-comings. Students of 17 are mature enough to know when they are being sold short. They are not prepared to be fobbed off with unprepared lectures, unmarked work, poor teaching, frequent cancellation of lessons, lack of interest in either the subject or themselves.

The almost unassailable tenure of the incompetent or feckless teacher must go. But it will not do to attack teachers for lack of professionalism if they are treated as ushers and monitors. The result of one hundred years of such treatment has been a trades unionism that protects the idle and inadequate provided they do not break the criminal law:

This is the antithesis of professionalism and ultimately blocks the rightful demand for accountability from government, the LEA, parents, pupils, governors and colleagues.[12]

Tertiary colleges are few in number and have to make their way in the world. The spotlight is upon them. They are studied by those who see in them a pattern and hope for the future and by others who fear them as threatening an established order. The author, working as he does in the only tertiary college in the capital, some 10 miles from the British Council and the Department of Education and Science, has to contend with more than a fair share of official and overseas scrutiny. The Minister of Education of the People's Republic of China, Jiang Nanxiang, whose own responsibility extends to 90 million children in infant schools alone, visited in 1979 an 'Oxbridge' Science class and a bricklaying one, and commented, 'This is what education should be'. We still wonder if he thought that at the next hour the two sets would change places. This remark has left us suitably chastened by the realisation that we still have a long way to go before tertiary ideals are fully realised.

Notes

1   'School Education in England—Problems and Initiatives', *Times Educational Supplement,* 15 Oct. 1976

2   MacDonald, B., 'Accountability Standards and the Process of Schooling' in Becher, T. and Maclure, S. (eds.), *Accountability in Education* (Slough, NFER, 1978), chap. 6

3   Kogan, M., 'Institutional Autonomy and Public Accountability' in *Autonomy and Accountability in Educational Administration* (London, British Educational Administration Society, Nov. 1975) p.19

4   Ellis, T., *et al. William Tyndale—The Teachers' Story* (London, Writers and Readers Publishing Co-operative, 1976) p.12

5   Kogan, M., *op.cit.,* p.21

6   Evidence presented by LEA associations to the Macfarlane Committee, reported in *Times Higher Education Supplement,* 7 (385) (1980), 1

7   Moore, D., in response to Kogan, M., *op.cit.,* pp.32 – 6

8   *Teacher Education and Training:* James Report (London, HMSO, 1971)

9   These two letters, written by J. F. Lambert, Chairman of the Education Committee, London Borough of Richmond upon Thames, are reprinted with his kind permission and the permission of the two newspapers

10 Gent, C. and Scammels, L., *The Administration of Technical Colleges* (Manchester, Manchester University Press, 1971), p.79
11 Becher, T. and Maclure, S., *op.cit.* (note), 'Accounting Procedures and Educational Processes', p.225
12 Ellis, A., in response to Kogan, M. *op.cit.,* p.32

7

ADULT AND CONTINUING EDUCATION: LIFE-LONG LEARNING

A. B. Cotterell

Adult education in England and Wales is a palimpsest. Current provision is in the hands of numerous formal and informal bodies whose areas of operation and levels of activity have been often drawn and redrawn on the educational map. Even within the sector of prime interest here, namely that under the control of Local Education Authorities, earlier arrangements are not infrequently effaced to make room for a newer pattern of organisation. It appears to some adult educators that the service provided for their students is always adjusted to suit the rest of the education system, whether compulsory or post-compulsory. Local Education Authorities exhibit a bewildering display of both provision and commitment. This diversity was acknowledged in 1973 by the Russell Report, though it firmly recommended that Local Education Authorities take the initiative in establishing area organisations which would eliminate unnecessary overlap and competition.[1]

To understand the part a tertiary college might be expected to play in what is a very complex pattern it is necessary to examine the palimpsest, carefully noting both the original writing and later alterations to the manuscript. Such an historical approach should elucidate the origins and growth of the various organisations involved in adult education as well as their relationship to each other. It might also help us to see adult and continuing education against the perspective of change we call life in the twentieth century.

Although adult education is far down the list of priorities for public expenditure—in December 1979 the TUC General Secretary, Mr Len Murray, accused the Conservative administration of 'abdicating all responsibility for this important sector of education'—there remains a strong native tradition of learning for the mature student, whatever the motivation or level of attainment. Its resilience can be discerned in two institutions founded during the past decade. The first, the Open University, was created by Royal Charter in 1969 but only began teaching its first 20000 students in 1971. As Peter Calvocoressi has remarked:

> The Open University was one of the great inventions of this period and a testimony of the continuing vitality of Britain. Between the wars the cultural scene had been enriched first by the BBC and then by Penguin Books and it was a heartening symptom to observe that as those institutions lost much of their pre-eminent purpose and flavour something else new emerged from the British genius.[2]

The other radical departure of the 1970s was the Adult Literacy Campaign. This movement was a national ground swell of educational awareness caused by world turmoil over adult illiteracy. Between 1950 and 1970 the number of literate adults increased from 879 millions to 1504 millions. While the actual number of illiterates increased by 83 millions to 738 millions during the same period of time, the percentage of illiterates in the world dropped from 44.3 per cent in 1950 to 34.2 per cent in 1970. UNESCO-sponsored schemes in the 1960s were aimed at supporting economic and social development in the Third World. It came therefore as a surprise to many Britons that between one and two million of their fellow adults were also without reading and writing skills. The public response to the call for volunteer tutors was unprecedented. Enough volunteers were trained in rudimentary teaching techniques by 1975 for some 100000 adult students to be receiving individual tuition. In this unusual enterprise the media played a crucial role. Programmes not only assisted adult literacy learners and their volunteer tutors but more they helped identify those persons in need of tuition by providing a confidential referral service. As with the Open

University, television and radio brought serious study into homes that in an earlier generation would have lost contact with formal learning at the statutory school leaving age. In the process adult education shed a little of its preference for non-examinable courses and came nearer to the idea of continuing or recurrent education.

A philosophy for basic adult education could be discovered in the writings of Paulo Freire, who in north-eastern Brazil had devised programmes designed to emancipate the peasants from the personal and community constraints of illiteracy. 'To alienate men from their own decision-making', asserted Freire, 'is to change them into objects'.[3] Functional literacy—those reading and writing abilities needed by an individual in order to have a satisfying and effective life in the community—was recognised belatedly not to be fixed or stationary. What is demanded of a person relates to changing social and economic conditions. The illiterate or semi-illiterate adult is particularly vulnerable, though the swiftness of change is obliging 'educated' people to constantly update their knowledge. The upward trend of functional literacy in developed countries has caused an American commentator to coin a new phrase: 'technological literacy'.[4] Admission of the need to tackle this fundamental problem was made at the very moment Mr Murray expressed fears for the future of the adult education service. It was announced in the House of Commons that £500000 would be used for the development of an Adult Literacy and Basic Skills Unit.

From 1919 to 1973

The two key inscriptions on the palimpsest of adult education in England and Wales this century are government reports. One is *The Adult Education Report,* issued on behalf of the Ministry of Reconstruction in 1919; the other is the report of the Russell Committee, entitled *Adult Education: A Plan for Development* and published in 1973. Between these seminal documents the present adult education service evolved.

The Ministry of Reconstruction at the end of the First World War voiced in its recommendations the aspiration of those people who wanted an extramural university education. Prior to the outbreak of hostilities the universities of Oxford, Cambridge and London were assisted by local colleges in providing extension lectures. The subjects offered covered the arts, science, social studies and philosophy. From 1903 the Workers' Educational Association had taken the lead in bringing university lectures and tutorials to the general public. The aim of the WEA was to join together those organisations interested in the needs of working men for higher education—the trades unions, the co-operative societies, and the universities. In 1907 the Board of Education was represented at the annual conference at Oxford and soon the universities followed the Association in seeking out students nationally. The number was small—less than 4000 in 1914—but no longer should a Jude vainly pen a plea for instruction in Greek to the head of an Oxford college.

The Adult Education Report of 1919 proposed the establishment of 'extramural departments', whose task was the liberal education of adult students. In addition to staff within the university, resident tutors were to be provided in those districts where there was sufficient extra-mural work or where such work could be started. Funding was the joint responsibility of central and local government.

The 1919 Report sought to meet the growing demand for adult education. Though it failed to erect a structure in which all levels of post-compulsory learning could flourish, the impetus behind its recommendations brought into existence a variety of provision. There was a gradual development of extra-mural departments, the growth of the WEA, the expansion of classes run by Local Education Authorities, and the foundation of voluntary centres and associations. One unforeseen consequence of extra-mural study was the elevation of full-time university education into the norm for young adults.

In 1907 two-thirds of the students at Sheffield University were evening students. In the 1960s the Open University was thought to be novel in basing itself on distance learning and non-residential study. The harnessing of the media was revolutionary. Harold Wilson's suggestion for a University of the Air drew widespread criticism in 1963—an unmistakable sign that an academic shake-up was required. The British had forgotten that university education was never exclusively full-time. Whilst the advantages of residential study for the 17 to 22 year-old student are manifest, the ability of the motivated part-timer to complete the same course over a longer period of time cannot be gainsaid. Campus-consciousness is not solely an American phenomenon.

Even today there are quite large numbers of part-time students in British universities registered for undergraduate level awards. The figure for 1979 – 80 is just under 4000. The great concentration is in London, notably at Birkbeck College. Where mid-career education has been looked upon as an institutional duty, especially in post-experience courses run by specialist university institutes and since 1965 by the new polytechnics, an extension of part-time provision is noticeable. But the financial and organisational pressures to concentrate on full-time students are as severe in higher adult education as elsewhere in post-compulsory education.

A complicating factor in the full-time/part-time debate is the esteem in which non-vocational adult education has been held. The sentiment goes deep. A recent expression was the terms of reference given to the Russell Committee: its members were asked to investigate only 'the provision of non-vocational adult education in England and Wales'. This restriction of outlook was originally formulated in the 1919 Report, which spoke of 'adult education (other than technical and vocational)'. The distinct lack of concern for examinations may be commendable in a society increasingly preoccupied with pieces of paper rather than education as a means of personal fulfilment, but a consequence is that in contrast to other countries adult education in Britain does not refer to the education of adults as opposed to the education of children. The emphasis on non-vocational study precludes an holistic approach to adult learning. It accounts for the diversity of providers, the absence of overall planning, and the poverty of examinations devised for adult students.

The antithesis between education for the world of work and education for leisure is now less easy to sustain. Despite the narrowness of its terms of reference, the Russell Committee argued for the right of access to qualifications. 'Adult education programmes', the Report concluded, 'should provide opportunities for adults to complete secondary, further and higher education and offer access to qualifications at all levels.' Paragraphs 286 – 299 dealt with access to qualification and in its range of re-commendations underlined the urgent case for rationalisation. The recommendations were as follows:

> Increasingly adult education should provide opportunities by day and in the evening for adults who wish to improve their capacity for study, to

extend their formal education or to prepare themselves for achieving a qualification.

In an age of occupational mobility adult education should help people to clarify their choices before transferring to a second or a third career and should assist the process of transfer by preparing for entry to the training needed.

The experiments being made by certain GCE examining boards in devising courses of a more flexible character and forms of assessment more appropriate to adults should be encouraged.

Universities and other bodies who offer academic or professional recognition should create opportunities for adult students to obtain their awards by part-time study and should expand such opportunities where they already exist.

The Committee of Vice-Chancellors and Principals, the Council for National Academic Awards and the Committee of Directors of Polytechnics should be invited to consider ways by which a transferable credit structure for degrees and other awards might be introduced and, with the Open University, the possibility of combined courses.[5]

The sweep is from basic education, or return to learning courses, to post-graduate study. Though the recommendations of the report as a whole amount to recommending a modest expansion of what is already in existence, the implication of a future policy of access to qualification is more radical and far-reaching. At every level of post-compulsory education there will have to be greater cooperation between educational institutions, examining bodies, employers, and the community. Possibly the advocacy of special provision for disadvantaged adults by the Russell Committee is the only other recommendation likely to be retained on the palimpsest.

The Cinderella of adult education between 1919 and 1973 has been the service offered by Local Education Authorities. Its origins are to be located in the late nineteenth century, though formal acknowledgement was only made in the 1902 Education Act and the 1919 Report. Evening institutes comprised the chief mode of operation, but in the 1920s the first centres were opened in separate buildings. London established 'Literary Institutes', even giving in 1939 the City Literary Institute purpose-built premises.

Another pioneering LEA was Cambridgeshire through the inspiration of Henry Morris, the Director of Education from 1922 till 1954. Morris was worried about rural depopulation and sought to arrest the drift to the towns by means of Village Colleges. A village college was planned as a secondary school, a library, and an adult

When Half Life has a Human Dimension

Sir, — A sinister mutation has appeared here in Cumbria. It is called a half person.

Half persons are the poor — and most of them are OAPs, the unemployed and retired people — who cannot afford to pay full fees for winter educational and leisure classes run by the educational authorities.

A concrete instance, is my own small art class. This year the class has been cancelled for lack of support. Although it has about 10 people, the education authorities say there are only five people, not enough for a class. In their eyes if

you can't afford the full fee you are only half a person.

In effect, if you haven't enough money to pay for your education you aren't a human being — merely a half-person and as such, you don't warrant human culture.

Joan Eadington.
Watermillock,
Penrith, Cumbria.
Guardian
31-10-79

Fig. 7.1 'The Cinderella of adult education'.
(Reproduced by kind permission of *The Guardian*.)

education centre, serving an area of about 10 000 people. According to Morris, it would 'as the community centre of the neighbourhood . . . provide for the whole man, and abolish the duality of education and ordinary life.'[6] The concept was an original one. It avoided the non-vocational/vocational divide by lumping together all the educational services available to those above the age of 11. At the time of local government reorganisation the old Cambridgeshire authority had built 10 Village Colleges.

The years immediately after the Second World War were a time of growth for adult education. In 1946 the Educational Settlements Association, an organisation founded in 1920 as a link between democratically run adult education institutions, was compelled to change its name to the Educational Centres Association. It recognised the increasing diversity of centre work, particularly as several Local Education Authorities following Morris' example sponsored centres and residential colleges. The foundation of colleges of further education also brought another major institution into the field, especially where a department of adult education was created. The expansion of adult learning is borne out in attendance figures. Whereas in 1960 the proportion of young people of 17 or under attending evening institutes was 31.7 per cent of students enrolled, in 1969 the percentage had declined to 16.8. Nearly 1.7 million students over the age of 18, or one in 20 of the adult population, attended Local Education Authority classes in 1968 – 69. This was six times the number of adults in university extra-mural and WEA classes. The number continued to rise in the early 1970s until fee increases caused the start of a decline. Between 1975 – 76 and 1976 – 77 the fall-off was probably 11 per cent.[7]

After Russell

The official response to *Adult Education: A Plan for Development* has been unpropitious. It is lost in the pending tray at the Department of Education and Science. Public expenditure cuts, falling rolls, and argument over the core curriculum have ensured its neglect. Yet this fate hardly comes as a surprise. The Russell Committee was too rooted in the non-vocational outlook to break with tradition, escape from the confines of its terms of reference, and insist upon an integrated system of adult learning. The device of setting up the Advisory Council for Adult and Continuing Education as a stop gap, even an alternative to action, bodes ill for future development. The Advisory Council has been told that it will be continued till 1983, but only an unreflecting optimist expects that its work might result in facilitating structural improvement. Even if the policies and priorities necessary for the evolution of a coherent pattern of provision in tune with present and future requirements are identified, there is no guarantee that the government of the day will be interested in their adoption. And it is apparent that without central direction no fundamental change is possible.

In the meantime adult educators are finding themselves facing great difficulties. From 1975 onwards most Local Education Authorities put up course fees, some to an economic level. They did so because fees are one of the few items in the education budget over which they have complete control. Numbers of students enrolled have fallen and in certain parts of the country adult education has largely disappeared.

The rundown of provision is abetted by the imprecision of the relevant legislation. The 'large and important place in the development of adult education' envisaged for Local Education Authorities in the 1919 Report was incorporated in the 1944 Education Act in the statutory duty placed on every LEA to provide adequate facilities for further education. Apart from full-time and part-time education for persons over compulsory school age, further education was defined as:

> leisure-time occupation, in such organised cultural training and recreational activities as are suited to their requirements, for any persons over compulsory school age who are able and willing to profit by the facilities provided for the purpose.[8]

Unscrupulous Local Education Authorities have taken advantage of the vagueness of 'occupation' to substitute the hiring of facilities for structured learning. While there is room for self-directed study and a workshop approach, a survey published in 1978 found that adult educators were agreed on the importance of teaching.[9] The Russell Committee had felt constrained to point out the anomalous position of the service and recommend that the 1944 Act be amended so that it would be unlawful for a LEA to use as an economy measure the suspension of adult education courses. Its aim was 'to secure a clear commitment from central government as to the place of adult education as an essential element in the national system of education'.[10]

How far short of the target the recommendation fell can be seen in the letter Mr Murray sent to the Prime Minister in December 1979. He informed Mrs Thatcher that:

> Almost 40 LEAs have already raised their fees for evening classes and more Authorities will be doing so in the near future. Other areas have

reduced their adult education programmes, in some cases so that no provision remains. Some Authorities are closing adult education centres, reducing the evenings on which centres are open for courses, or failing to renew the contracts of staff. Indeed, in some areas services have been cut so drastically that potential students are no longer given the opportunity to enrol in courses even if they are able and willing to pay increased fees.

It is becoming abundantly clear that the spending cuts are hitting adult education so hard that there are real fears in some areas that it could virtually cease to exist unless steps are taken to safeguard it . . . It is our view that the Government has a duty to ensure that adult education remains a viable part of our total education provision and, at the least, to impress on Local Education Authorities their obligation to retain the structure of adult education as it has developed since 1944.[11]

Adult education, as provided by the Local Education Authorities, is threatened. The other two main providers—the WEA and the universities—are also constrained by financial cutback. Yet it is at this moment of crisis today that we need to review and develop better adult learning systems. A new comprehensive approach is as urgent for older adults as it is for the young adults of the 16 to 19 age group.

A New Concept of Adult Education

The post-1945 world has forced a reassessment of reality on most adults. Not only have traditional occupations altered or disappeared, but also social and moral standards were modified by the increasing tempo of technological change. Adult students often suffer from the 'difficulty of disengagement', or the struggle to relinquish previous knowledge, in learning new skills, so that it is not unusual for people to feel uncertain and insecure when they have to unlearn some of the attitudes instilled into them through their own upbringing. Apart from emotional flexibility and resilience, an adult requires sufficient new knowledge and skills to face and adapt to future uncertainty without losing a sense of identity. Impermanence is already the accepted experience of the young, who take for granted the constantly diminishing gap between a scientific discovery and its large-scale application. 'More than 90 per cent of scientists and inventors in all human history', a recent UNESCO report pointed out, 'are living in our times'.[12] It might be said that education is preparing people for societies which do not yet exist. Urging a firm linkage of 'school and out-of-school education', the same report, entitled *Learning to Be*, comments:

There are many possible definitions of adult education. For a very large number of adults in the world today, it is a substitute for the basic education they missed. For the many individuals who received only a very incomplete education, it is the complement to elementary or professional education. For those whom it helps to respond to new demands which their environment makes on them, it is the prolongation of education. It offers further education to those who have already received high-level training. And it is the means of individual development for everybody. One or other of these aspects may be more important in one country than in another, but they all have their validity. Adult education can no longer be limited to rudimentary levels, or confined to 'cultural' education for a minority.[13]

Cited as a model of adult education provision are the so-called 'workers universities' of Yugoslavia (open-access institutions with individually devised courses) and the national system of Sweden, where two out of every six adults take part.

Change is faster today. Technology is reshaping our intellectual world. Knowledge is no longer a slowly evolving phenomenon, nor is it particularly confined to specialist fields of activity. Satellite communications and computer-aided storage and retrieval of information have made an awareness of change and of new possibilities something which is generally shared by people living in technologically advanced countries. Education, however, in Europe has hardly adjusted to these new conditions, though a radical proposal was put forward in the 1970s. Education is still seen as a terminal apprenticeship for a working life. According to a report published in 1973 by the Organisation for Economic Cooperation and Development (OECD):

> The advanced societies of the twentieth century have behaved as if education could be expanded to the point where all available talents would be developed, and that the schools would thereby become one of the main avenues to greater social equity. The path to this state of social justice based on education has been seen as a continuous and lengthening process including pre-primary, primary, secondary and higher education.[14]

To counter this tendency the OECD offered the 'concept of recurrent education . . . namely that education opportunities should be spread out over an individual's lifetime, *as an alternative* to the ever-lengthening period of continuing education for youth'.[15] Such a model implies the alternation of education with other activities, of which the principal would be work, but which might also include leisure and retirement. For recurrent education to embrace the working population a policy of educational leave of absence would have to be established by means of appropriate incentives. And during youth education would have to present wider and more flexible options: work experience, social service, and organised leisure pursuits as part of the learning process.

The corollary would be that post-compulsory students possessed a right to voluntary deferred opportunities for education, whether further, higher or adult (to use British terms). They would permanently own an educational future, though in that future education might be more self-directed learning in association with advanced communication systems.

The arguments deployed against the lengthening of 'schooling' are several. First, there is the 'malaise' in secondary education, especially the experience of France. Connected with this disenchantment, on the part of both staff and students, is the continuation of the learning process long after physical maturation is complete. In primitive societies there are rituals specifically designed to initiate the mature youth into the adult community at the earliest opportunity. GCE examinations seem rather poor substitutes. Moreover, from the point of view of personality development, isolation from the challenges of life outside the protective educational environment appears undesirable. The completion of a first degree usually occurs at the end of the 17 years of full-time education.

Another reason advanced for periodicity in learning is the emerging imbalance between supply and demand of highly qualified manpower. Economic and social factors clearly influence student choice. Higher education is insulated from neither intellectual fashion nor job expectations, as underutilised faculties of Classics and Engineering serve to remind us today. The further expansion of a formal and youth-oriented post-compulsory education system will not solve the problem of supply and demand. It could well be argued that a disproportionate amount of money has been spent on compulsory education in the last few decades. In addition, the increasing staying-on rate after 16 years of age as well as the increasing going-on rate to higher education have ensured that remaining resources have been overwhelmingly concentrated on the under-24 year olds. For present-day 35 to 55 year-olds an educational 'generation gap' probably exists. To a lesser extent, a knowledge disability is shared by all adults whose education did not include 'learning how to learn'. A response to the knowledge explosion which comprises no more than increasing both the volume of information to be absorbed and the number of years spent in formal education can hardly be called a preparation for the modern world. As Basil Bernstein remarked of the secondary curriculum:

> For the mass of the population the framing is tight . . . The evaluative system places an emphasis upon attaining *states* of knowledge rather than *ways* of knowing.[16]

The exploratory habit is not entirely instinctive. People can lose a desire for knowledge. They can unlearn curiosity. At the crudest level, a large vocabulary is a mere word-list unless one has developed the intellectual ability to search out new meanings.

Recurrent education, its advocates argue, can remedy the shortcomings of the present educational system and meet future needs. Whether or not we agree with such claims, it is evident that the advantages of modifying the end-on model of primary, secondary and higher education are numerous. From the very beginning of post-compulsory education we could design a structure to meet the changing needs of a life-time. Further, adult and higher education would then be perceived as a single sector dealing with the over-16s. The peculiar division of educational provision between the various government departments might be brought to a sensible end. How can the country respond to economic variation when education and training are divorced? At the moment Industry Training Boards, the Manpower Services Commission, and the Department of Education and Science go their separate ways. Often the college of further education is the battlefield for their rival schemes. The casualty is of course the student, like the ITB apprentice who is unable to participate in college minority activities with young adults on other courses between 8.45 am and 5.30 pm daily. He is the terminal apprentice, a relic of the ancient guilds.

The importance of the idea of recurrent education is the liberating effect it will have on attitudes towards post-compulsory provision. Doubtless its progress will be organic, growing in those institutions which welcome it. One of these will be the tertiary college. The starting point for reorientation of policy must be the treatment of the 16 to 19 age group. Only in places where education for the young adult is not merely a headlong rush into university or polytechnic will there be a likelihood of recycling learning. An effective institutional model could well prove to be the tertiary college, possessed as it often is of a comprehensive range of full-time courses for the 16 to 20 year-olds, a number of specialist part-time day courses serving local industry and commerce, an extensive adult education programme for vocational and non-vocational students, and effective links with employers and higher education, including the Open University.

The Way Ahead

The guiding principle of recurrent education is the fundamental right of an individual to decide his own future. It presupposes adaptation and emancipation. The student is permitted varying degrees of commitment to study as well as various patterns of attendance. Such an approach to continuing education requires adequate counselling and guidance, but then teachers of the 16 to 19 age group have become painfully aware of a similar need too. The academic pathways are becoming less certain, and consequently students look for careers guidance which relates to the whole range of employment and educational opportunities.

The tertiary organisation proposed elsewhere in this book as a solution to the problem of the 16 to 19 age group could at local level provide an efficient base, or centre, for an adult and continuing education system cast in the recurrent mould (see Fig. 7.2). It alone of post-compulsory institutions has an holistic potential. There are, however, dangers in the 'all-eggs-in-one-basket' solution and these are particularly dangerous for the tradition of participatory adult education fostered by the ECA movement. Conflict already exists in colleges of further education which have a substantial commitment to adult education. As one head of department put it:

> I think that this is what will kill adult education in the Further Education College, the academic boards. They're the second biggest problem, I think. The first one is the County which is just insensitive to the effects of fee structures. But . . . I think in the long term we will look back upon academic boards as being ways of blowing your nose at the local population, because academic boards are interested in vocational and mainly full-time courses.[17]

In so far as the academic board is an arena in which departments

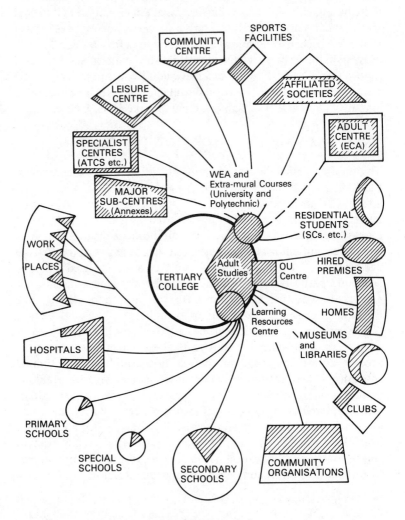

Fig. 7.2 An area organisation for adult and continuing
education centred on a Tertiary College. Shaded areas
indicate location of learning.

compete for resources and where decisions are taken about their allocation, the diverse learning requests of the over-20s are likely to get short shrift. The view of such a body inevitably tends to be 16 to 19 oriented. A strong principal can redress the balance, but a more secure method of management via the governing body is essential, even if it involves some erosion of institutional and teacher autonomy. Participation by the community in the running of tertiary colleges which are developing a recurrent education programme cannot be avoided. Recurrent education institutions, serving the community irrespective of age, must be responsible to the local community as much as to the Local Education Authority.

Another danger of an oversize recurrent education campus is the institutionalisation of community activities. We do not want what Colin Ball has termed 'a hypermarket of corporate life, . . . available to those who can get there, and who are prepared to fight the inevitable bureaucracies that will grow to administer it'.[18] While Henry Morris may have favoured the village shop, we are obliged to seek a model suited to the increasingly urban environment of the final decades of the twentieth century. We need to combine the advantages of centralised resources with the accessibility of local centres. We need the community use of all learning facilities in a coordinated and purposeful manner—a network, an area of organisation of the kind recommended in the Russell Report. In the tertiary college there would have to be an area head, a director of studies or a head of department, who would be responsible for both educational provision and administration in the catchment area. Besides using major sub-centres and schools, the area head would develop other appropriate facilities throughout the area. It would be logical to return to Local Education Authorities in Counties responsibility for leisure, since at the moment both District Councils and New Town Development Corporations busily compete with LEA adult education. Sports halls, sports pitches, theatres, cinemas and swimming pools would then be available for a coherent programme of courses as well as individual and club use. Where participatory adult education already exists at centres within the catchment area, a mutually satisfactory relationship would have to be established. But the prior existence of a local tradition of education management by adult students must be a bonus for recurrent education, which prizes the freedom of the student to learn what he will when he will. Within the tertiary college at least we envisage the creation of learning resource centres, utilising less mass media than locally available electronic aids for individual or group tuition. It has been suggested that these materials could be prepared by a national agency concerned with recurrent education.[19] Many unsolved questions remain. Certification or accreditation; evaluation; the share of costs between employers and tax-payers; the management of recurrent education institutions. But even in the timid recommendations of the Russell Report the concept of life-long learning is already inherent. It may not be long before the Department of Education and Science has to relate basic education to a coherent scheme of educational opportunities throughout life. Knowledge keeps no better than fish. As the Open University Committee on Continuing Education succinctly said of our economic decline:

> . . . a substantial provision of continuing education is vital to the well-being of this country—not only for the personal lives of innumerable individual citizens, but because *their* understanding of the issues involved and *their* willingness to cooperate in essential tasks are vital to the future economic recovery and social well-being of this country.[20]

Notes

1   *Adult Education: A Plan for Development:* Report of the Committee of Inquiry under the Chairmanship of Sir Lionel Russell (London, HMSO, 1973), para.195
2   Calvocoressi, P., *The British Experience 1945 – 75* (Harmondsworth, Penguin, 1979) p. 164
3   Freire, P., *Pedagogy of the Oppressed* (Harmondsworth, Penguin, 1972), p.58
4   Quoted in Downing, J. (ed.), *Comparative Reading, Cross-National Studies of Behaviour and Processes in Reading and Writing* (London, Macmillan, 1973), p.247
5   Russell Report, *op.cit.* (note 1), p.xvii
6   Morris, H., *A Memorandum on the Provision of Educational and Social Facilities for the Countryside with Special Reference to Cambridgeshire, 1929,* p.3 (unpublished)
7   Mee, G. and Wiltshire, H., *Structure and Performance in Adult Education* (London, Longmans, 1978), p.98
8   *1944 Education Act* (London, HMSO, 1944), sect.44
9   Mee, G. and Wiltshire, H., *op.cit.,* chap. 3
10 Russell Report, *op.cit.* (note 1), pp.52-3
11 Quoted in *Education* pp.673 – 4 (21/28 December 1979)

12 *Learning to Be.* The Report of the International Commission on the Development of Education chairman Edgar Faure (London, Harrap, (for UNESCO), 1972), p.187
13 *ibid.,* p.205
14 *Recurrent Education: A Strategy for Lifelong Learning,* (Paris Centre for Educational Research and Innovation, 1973), p.5
15 *ibid.,* p.5
16 Bernstein, B., 'Classification and Framing of Educational Knowledge', *Class, Codes and Control. Vol. 1: Theoretical Studies Towards a Sociology of Language* (London, Routledge and Kegan Paul, 1971), p.214
17 Mee, G. and Wiltshire, H., *op.cit.,* p.69
18 Ball, C., 'Hypermarkets of Corporate Life', *Times Educational Supplement,* 29 November 1974, p.2
19 Fowler, G., 'Towards recurrent education in Britain' in Houghton, V. and Richardson, K. (eds.) *Recurrent Education* (London, Ward Lock Educational, 1974), p.134
20 *Report of the Committee on Continuing Education,* (Milton Keynes, Open Univ., Dec. 1976), p.83

8

LIBRARY AS LEARNING ENVIRONMENT

B. L. Pearce

Introduction

A tertiary library has a particular part to play in preparing students for the self-organisation required of them in higher education or their subsequent careers. It can provide experience in private study, guidance in the use of information sources and help in their evaluation, advice on assignment preparation and presentation, and practice in the effective use and disposition of personal time.

While the principal objective is to assist students with their studies, parallel with this there goes the purpose of enabling them to develop their own knowledge and abilities in later life; to be able to update themselves and widen their horizons, and to evaluate and compare opinions and ideas. This latter aim is in accord with many aspects of liberal education—in the post-war context: to equip students to exercise an independent and responsible role as citizens, as well as to enter into something of the cultural heritage, and to enjoy reading for personal interest and recreation.[1,2]

In a tertiary college, the implications of open entry will include the servicing of academic and vocational courses of the most diverse types and levels—some of high calibre and of a very demanding standard—together with meeting the requirements of post-graduate special courses and of staff updating and research. At the other extreme there will be courses of a more remedial nature where the achievement of basic literacy may be the prime objective. Additionally, there are likely to be the requirements of adult education courses, such as those of the Open University or which adopt the flexi-study approach. The meeting of these objectives, in the tertiary situation, will entail the need to accommodate divergent library and study traditions, and to allow for differences in the maturity of students and in their previous experience of libraries. This will affect, for example, the design of the building, and the qualities to be looked for in the library staff. Thus, though the services provided may not be unique to tertiary colleges, there will be considerable modifications in orientation and approach.

The services may be expected to include the following elements, each of which will be discussed in more detail in the main part of this chapter (see also Fig. 8.1):

Guidance. Tuition in library use and information sources; tutorial guidance and the supervision of assignment and essay preparation; advisory services—reference and bibliographical.

Accommodation and Facilities. Silent study and quiet discussion areas; audio/visual playback and viewing facilities; photocopying; accommodation for lecture, seminar, tutorial and project work.

Stock. Bookstock—for loan and reference; periodicals and abstracts, special collections, e.g. standards, projects, maps; audio/visual software.

Staff. Staff equipped to provide the tuition and advice; to supervise the study areas, and to select, classify, interpret and exploit the stock over the wide subject range involved.

A major concern is to bring to the attention of users (and potential users) the range of these materials and services in the library and the way that they may be utilised. The key role in this task, and in integrating the library's function with the educational programme of the college, is played by:

Tuition in library use

At Richmond upon Thames College, a basic four-lecture library induction module has been implemented for students on both academic and vocational courses and at all levels of study. This consists of:

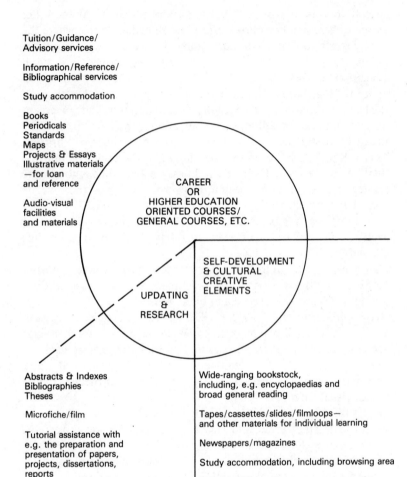

Tuition/Guidance/
Advisory services

Information/Reference/
Bibliographical services

Study accommodation

Books
Periodicals
Standards
Maps
Projects & Essays
Illustrative materials
—for loan
and reference

Audio-visual
facilities
and materials

CAREER
OR
HIGHER EDUCATION
ORIENTED COURSES/
GENERAL COURSES, ETC.

SELF-DEVELOPMENT
& CULTURAL
CREATIVE
ELEMENTS

UPDATING
&
RESEARCH

Abstracts & Indexes
Bibliographies
Theses

Microfiche/film

Tutorial assistance with
e.g. the preparation and
presentation of papers,
projects, dissertations,
reports

Study accommodation, including
carrels.

Wide-ranging bookstock,
including, e.g. encyclopaedias and
broad general reading

Tapes/cassettes/slides/filmloops—
and other materials for individual learning

Newspapers/magazines

Study accommodation, including browsing area

Tutorial guidance in, e.g. essay preparation
and creative writing

Cultural activities such as, e.g.
concerts, talks, exhibitions and displays/
Societies or groups, producing, e.g.
anthologies of staff-student writing

College magazine

Fig. 8.1 The library contribution to college objectives

Lecture I: Introduction to the lay-out of information sources in the Library and Resources Centre, and an outline of library procedures.

Lecture II: Principles of the classification scheme in use and the practice of information retrieval techniques via catalogue and indexes.

Lecture III: Introduction to general reference books.

Lecture IV: Exposition of information sources relevant to specific subject field including periodical indexes and abstracts, supporting collections in the Resources Centre, and loan/information services external to the college.

More specific lectures and seminars can be given to meet the requirements of TEC, BEC and, shortly, DATEC, and the module can be adapted to suit the needs of courses with individual requirements such as art and design, secretarial, and business studies, respectively. Expositions of the bibliographical background of a particular subject field can be given on, for instance, electrical engineering or English literature, and lectures and expositions are given to Open University preparatory course students. For students on general bridging and remedial courses, an appropriate module can be developed and given to smaller groups.

Group guidance on the techniques of information and bibliographical searching in connection with project/extended essay preparation is followed by tutorials on an individual basis. Developing from this the *tutorial* is an important aspect of the academic librarian's role and can involve supervision of essay/project preparation across the entire student spectrum. It can extend fruitfully to guidance on creative writing and presentation, or to other areas of staff specialism. The university tutorial system, whereby a small group of students may be interviewed jointly in regard to fact and presentation of a current assignment, could well be a model for a similar development within the tertiary system, in close parallel, as it is, with this tutorial supervision of individual students by the tertiary librarians. The one-to-one relationship is probably the more satisfactory, provided that staff time is available, but the use of the two approaches need not be mutually exclusive.

Integration

The integration of the library with the work and requirements of the college depends partly upon this teaching and related liaison of the college and tutor librarians, partly on the functional responsibility of the college librarian—including the need for his awareness of the development of academic board policy—and partly upon effective channels of communication and liaison. The latter can be of a formal or informal nature.

In many colleges there is a library committee where students and representatives of the subject teams can meet with the librarian who will normally act as chairman. However, this can involve considerable expenditure of time in the preparation of minutes and agendas, and a viable alternative is for representatives to be appointed but to liaise individually with the librarian and/or his subject specialists. This more relaxed and direct approach has been found to work well in the tertiary context. A library committee does have its virtues as a sounding-board, provided its role is seen to be advisory rather than functional and its deliberations are not confined to minutiae. In either case there will normally be some higher 'forum', be it the academic board or one of its committees, at which policy matters in connection with the library can be discussed.

Along with the college librarian's responsibilities to the principalship and academic board for the teaching and service functions of the library, there goes his necessary availability to any user or potential user of the library, be it student or staff, member of the public, local teacher or other enquirer who may wish to make recommendations or who comes for advice.

The advisory service, offering bibliographical and reference expertise, will require the services of all the academic and professional librarians, for there will certainly be more than one service-point to be manned in a large tertiary library. Some supervision of students will be necessary, and thus the need for maturity and a suitable temperament should be kept in mind during staff selection.

Resources

Accommodation

The preferred library accommodation will be a centralised complex on one site and should not be less than 1000 square metres in area. Additional to the book-shelving areas interspersed with study accommodation and a browsing/periodical display area, traditional to all educational libraries, there should be a learning resources area, or suite, for the wide range of audio-visual materials and equipment now an essential component of the educational process. Additional rooms should be provided for reserve bookstock, for audio-visual materials, and for back issues of periodicals. Seminar and lecture rooms will be needed for tuition in library use and supervision of project and assignment work, and the necessary general office accommodation will include an office for the college librarian, and offices and rest room for members of the library staff. Within the library there will be the usual issue desk, readers' advisory points, catalogues, display and book-exhibition areas and, a separate area for reference material. It is vital in a tertiary college library to effect a separation between the 'silent study' areas and those where quiet conversation is acceptable. Facilities for varied types of study pattern are advisable, and as conversation must necessarily occur around the issue and advisory desks and at the catalogue, more relaxed conditions can prevail in these areas. A specimen library design is shown in Fig. 8.2.

In 1976, closer to the commencement of the tertiary era, most of the libraries surveyed[3] were below the recommended minimum, but this was because the concept was in its infancy and some of the component institutions had their origin as smallish provincial colleges. The Richmond upon Thames College library and the Abraham Moss complex at Manchester both exceed 1000 square metres, and it is clear that the tertiary college library of the eighties will need to approximate to this accommodation area if it is to fulfil its function.

Stock

In a tertiary college library this will include books, pamphlets and reports, standards, maps, projects and essays, periodicals, and a wide range of audio-visual materials.

One of the outstanding features of tertiary college librarianship is the effect on finance and book-selection of the wide range of subjects and the variations of level and nature of provision needed within many of the individual subjects. The selection of bookstock will also need to take into account the variation in reading ability and previous educational pattern of the student population. There will

GROUND FLOOR

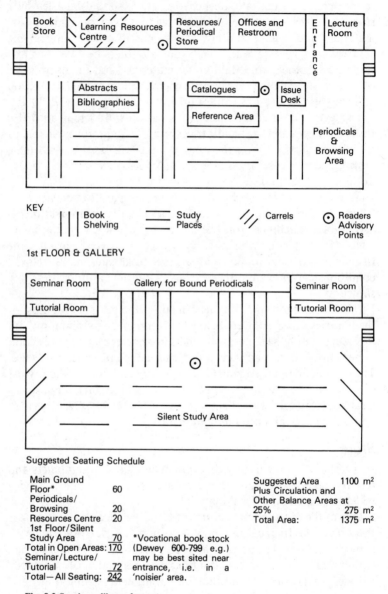

Suggested Seating Schedule

Main Ground
Floor*   60
Periodicals/
Browsing   20
Resources Centre   20
1st Floor/Silent
Study Area   70
Total in Open Areas: 170
Seminar/Lecture/
Tutorial   72
Total—All Seating: 242

Suggested Area   1100 m²
Plus Circulation and
Other Balance Areas at
25%   275 m²
Total Area: 1375 m²

*Vocational book stock
(Dewey 600-799 e.g.)
may be best sited near
entrance, i.e. in a
'noisier' area.

Fig. 8.2 Specimen library lay-out.

thus be a need not only for textbooks but for general back-ground and introductory material, a small proportion of which will be remedial. At the same time a comprehensive reference stock will be required and there will be the requirements too of special lecture courses, often at post-graduate level, as well as staff requirements for teaching purposes, updating, and research. Such provision can only be managed on a bookfund which is realistic and is meeting inflation. It has to be borne in mind that what constitutes a good stock today needs constant updating if it is to be a good stock in two years time.

For these reasons, the importance of the professional librarian's experience and expertise in book-selection becomes of increasing value. At Richmond upon Thames a subject specialisation scheme is in operation involving six members of the library team, and continuous stock-revision is necessary to meet the ever-shifting emphases of the courses.

It is recommended that multiple copies (up to a maximum of six) be purchased of standard textbooks in constant demand. At least one copy of all such items should be retained on reference or for short-term loan. Ultra-expensive and important out-of-print material should be relegated to the comparative safety of the librarian's office. Funding and staff time will be needed to implement and maintain a security system and, alternatively, if baggage is to be excluded, an area must be set aside for it and there arises the question of lockers or of supervision.

The bookstock at Richmond upon Thames—a group 7 college—amounts to 60 000 volumes, of which some 7000 are in reserve and another 7000 are semi-book materials. In the writer's view, no tertiary college library should be satisfied with less than 40 000 volumes; anything less would be inadequate to fulfil the wide range of requirements. Clearly, there will be cases in which this figure will need to be achieved over a period of years but initial setting-up grants can help to ease the transitional period.

Periodicals are an essential element of tertiary library stock. They contribute to current awareness in research, teaching and assignment work. They generate subject interest, and because of their presentation stimulate broad general reading and understanding of the contemporary scene. They will include journals, magazines and newspapers (some of which may be in foreign languages) and their appropriate abstracts. In relation to the mixed motivation/ability range of a tertiary college, their provision will be of especial value, and a list of about 300 titles is suggested. Much less will not provide a sufficient range to support courses, while much more will simply cost too much. In the light of rising costs, and in order to accommodate changing requirements, the list will need to be under revision at least annually.

Files of periodicals and newspapers are retained for a period depending on frequency of issue, availability of storage space, and demand. It is usual to retain current copies of periodicals on display racks in the library, and to loan only the non-current issues. Binding will only be resorted to for files which have to be retained permanently.

The *resources centre* is the area set aside for the housing and utilisation of audio-visual materials and equipment, together with audio-visual catalogues and indexes. This is an exciting and rapidly-developing area of library provision, used in support of an ever-increasing range of subjects by both students and staff. Audio materials include records, tapes, and cassettes. Provision must be made for playback facilities with headphones, preferably in semi-enclosed carrels. Visual media include slides, filmstrips and filmloops, microfilms, TV (off-air and video-cassette), illustrations, photographs, prints and reproductions, wallcharts, portfolios (such as the Jackdaw range) and OHP transparencies. Multi-media presentations may be tape-slide, filmstrip-cassette, or other permutations. Two or three wholly enclosed carrels will be desirable for film-loop or TV utilisation, typewriting, computer-based remedial learning, as well as for private study. Photocopying facilities may be provided here or, if practicable, at the library entrance.

The library role, with the advantages of its centralised location, open and manned for long hours, is to select, index, house and exploit learning resources software in its many forms and to provide viewing and play-back facilities for a variety of media. Utilisation is the keynote of this function.

Other units within the college will normally be responsible for the production or servicing of various types of learning resources or apparatus. Services which come readily to mind as flourishing at Richmond upon Thames are the audio-visual unit, where equipment can be booked out and maintained; the reprographic service for the production of teaching notes and other software; the closed circuit television (CCTV) unit, in conjunction with which the library has a monitor in a purpose-built carrel; a printing section, and the computing suite. Each of these facilities is under separate day-to-day management, the first two at technician level, and there is no formal provision for their interaction with the library or each other. This is an arrangement that, despite or because of its being unsystematised, has proved very satisfactory.

Finance

It must be stated at the outset that a bookfund of less than £20000 (1979 figures) is almost certain to be inadequate for a college in excess of 1500 F/T (or FTE) students. One method of calculation is to take a percentage of the college expenditure; something between 2 and 3 per cent, depending on size of college and level of work, is recommended by the Library Association, following the Parry Report. In practice the tertiary college librarian may count himself fortunate if, having done his sums, he finds himself with more than 1 per cent. Salaries and furniture/apparatus allocations will be budgeted separately.

Since the cost of books has risen so much in recent years, the purchasing power in real terms of a static sum is visibly reducing month by month. It must be appreciated that the bookfund has to cover not only books but periodicals, semi-book materials and audio-visual software, binding costs, stationery and sundries, inter-library loan charges and, possibly, small items of equipment. Periodical subscriptions are a substantial item and can easily absorb 25 per cent of the budget. This, when augmented by the other necessary charges, can leave only a little over half the total 'bookfund' for the purchase of actual books. The Librarian, however, should have virement over the global sum, as this will enable him to adjust his allocations to the various aspects in his spending during the course of the financial year. The amount available for books can then be divided between subject areas, but an allotment must be reserved for reference books and for the development of new courses.

Staff

Academic

The need to ensure the integration of the library with the college's teaching programme, and a full appreciation on the part of students of its potential for them, requires academic library staff, oriented and fitted for the liaison, coordination and teaching/tutorial work involved. If their enterprise is to be successful it will include involvement in college activities, both in the management committee structure—with membership of the academic board per DES *Circular 7/70*—and in diverse arts and other extra-curricular activities, as well as in the maintenance of external contacts and liaison.

Academic status is inherent in this function. It is essential if suitable staff are to be retained at the tertiary level, and if they are not to operate from a disadvantage in their day-to-day liaison in support of the college's educational objectives.

College librarian

The duties will include some teaching and tutorial work, though it is unlikely that a postholder will have time for many teaching hours since he will have responsibility for management, coordination and control over both the teaching and the service function of the library, besides participation in advisory duties, stock revision and book-selection in prescribed areas. Thus the job has many facets, combining as it does policy, liaison, educational and managerial elements. The post should be at least of senior lecturer grade and, in a college of any size, head of department or equivalent, as per Library Association[4] and NATFHE[5] documentation. The qualifications can include an academic degree, a teaching certificate, and a professional library qualification. The latter, rightly regarded as essential by most local authorities as well as the Library Association, will, in the long term, imply graduate status. Equally important is wide and substantial experience in the management of further education libraries. The truth is that, in common with many executive posts where the relationships and responsibilities are manifold, and/or not too rigidly defined, the job is what one makes it. It follows that *the* essential attributes are the accommodating benevolence of a Melanchthon combined with the diplomatic sagacity of a Machiavelli, but as rather few candidates may present themselves with these qualifications, in practice one has to choose from amongst those who apply.

Tutor-librarian/deputy librarian

This is a key role, round which the utilisation of the stock and service will pivot. In the situation where the college librarian is also tutor-librarian, a potential conflict of roles arises as it is difficult to coordinate the wide-ranging teaching/tutorial programme required in a tertiary college with expeditious administration of the library service. This problem is solved by the creation of a hybrid post with responsibility for the bulk of the teaching programme, while deputising, when necessary, for the college librarian. Such a postholder is also likely to be involved in considerable course and module preparation, and in extra-curricular activities. He will also share in the advisory duties, book-selection and stock revision of given areas of the bookstock. The post should be LII in all but the smallest colleges, and the appropriate qualifications would be substantially those for the college librarian.

Professional staff

The professional staff occupy a central position in the library service and should possess a professional qualification. Their duties include:

(a) Manning of the readers advisory points necessary for supervision as well as for bibliographical advice.

(b) Responsibility for book-selection, classification, cataloguing and stock-revision in prescribed areas of the bookstock; bibliographical searching, and listing.

(c) Specific functional or 'line' responsibilities , e.g.

(i) Reader services librarian—responsibility for coordinating book acquisition and processing; overall supervision of catalogue, lists of additions to stock; staff timetabling, and the loan, reference and bibliographical services.

(ii) Resources librarian—responsibility for the materials and equipment in the Resources area including selection, indexing, security and maintenance of the media, and for exploitation and dissemination by means of advice, displays, publications, and guidance to users and colleagues. It is necessary to appoint a keen and energetic person to this post, with an interest in new developments, if the full potential of a resources centre is to be realised. It is highly desirable that one or both these posts should be AP IV – V in order to obtain, and retain, staff of the right calibre.

(iii) Assistant librarians—It is recommended that there be at least two more professional librarians in a tertiary college library. In addition to their share of selection, classification, stock responsibility, considerable readers' advisory work and bibliographical searching, the postholders will divide between them specific responsibilities such as inter-library loans and reservations; the periodicals holdings, and certain of the special collections.

Support staff

Library assistants, normally on clerical grades, share the manning of the issue desk between them, and a main requirement is experience in routine library work with, for a small proportion of the posts, typing and/or accounting ability as well. In addition to the clerical work involved in ordering and receiving books, and the processing of the bookstock and audio-visual materials, their duties will include overdue notification, periodicals filing and display, support in the resources centre, library accounts and correspondence.

In a large tertiary library it is unlikely that less than three library assistants will suffice, and the possibility of designating at least one post as senior library assistant should be considered.

Where the college does not provide an audio-visual servicing unit or central porterage and maintenance services, technical or manual staff will also be required, but cleaning and caretaking services can normally be assumed at tertiary level.

For the total establishment the Library Association's recommendation of one member of the library staff to every 20 members of the teaching staff of the college (1:20) is a good general guide.[6] A specimen staff structure is shown in Fig. 8.3.

Inaugural Considerations

It is vital to the successful and smooth introduction of the new service that a college librarian-designate be appointed some 6 – 12 months before the tertiary college commences its operations. In the case of Richmond upon Thames this was done—by nomination from amongst the existing postholders—some ten months ahead of the starting date. This provided time and breathing space, as well as the requisite authority, for the necessary consultations and arrangements in regard to the merging of the bookstocks, catalogues and other facilities of the three services; the planning for their physical removal and assembly since they were each several miles apart; agreement on a staff establishment in the various categories discussed above; and for the planning of accommodation provision in advance of need. Consultation in regard to the establishment and accommodation requirements for efficient library management and use are vital if happy and practicable solutions are to be adopted but that such 'consultations' may sometimes be perfunctory is a well appreciated fact of life.

As in all mergers, human feelings come into the picture. Only one tertiary college librarian can be appointed, for example, from the two or three school or college librarians who may have been involved before. Naturally, there is potential for uncertainty and tension on several sides, and this will call for tact and understanding in everyday relationships and in the exercise of control. Inaugurally, the problem is best defused by identifying distinct, attractive and responsible roles for the colleagues disadvantaged by the change and, where possible, allowing them a large measure of autonomy in the discharge of these functions. Fortunately, the larger staff—and necessary supervision—and the wider work—and responsibility-load of the tertiary library, affords opportunity as well as necessity for the creation of these roles. The 'subject specialisation' referred to earlier can also be seen as a contribution to professional fulfilment and job satisfaction.

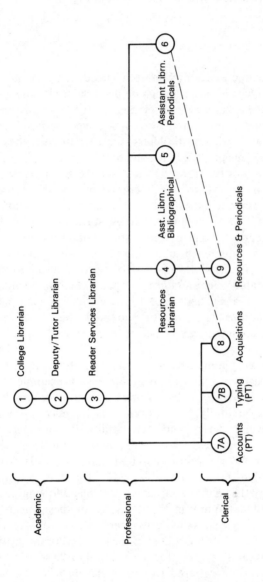

Posts 1–2 share the teaching/tutorial work with their managerial, advisory and liaison duties.
Posts 3–6 combine advisory and subject specialisation duties with their 'line' functions, as specified in the text.
Post 3 (and possibly 4) should be on a scale appropriate to its supervisory responsibilities.
Posts 7–9 share the manning of the issue desk as one of their main tasks.

Fig. 8.3 A specimen staff structure

Tertiary and Community

It is axiomatic that the function of a tertiary college library is to see itself in a community role and to offer its services to the locality. These may include information services utilising, as appropriate, computerised bases; loan and reference services to local teachers; the offer of tuition in library use to teachers, users of the public library, and students on adult education courses. Experience has shown that the latter benefit considerably from the library's specialised resources and from tuition in bibliographical use, as from the laboratories, computer facilities and CCTV likely to be available in adjacent areas in a tertiary college. Other natural involvements with local cultural affairs could include local history and literature, housing of archives, arrangement of exhibitions and displays.

A bibliographical centre may be built up using, where possible, existing academic and professional staff scholarship, and encouraging research and publication perhaps related to one or two carefully selected subject specialisations. More immediate scope is offered by publications such as college magazines and anthologies, edited by the library staff and sponsored by the college, which can encourage the production of creative and scholarly work.

Notes

1 Rothblatt, S., Tradition and Change in English Liberal Education, (London, Faber, 1976), pp. 9 – 10, 195 – 206
2 Pearce, B. L., Liberal education and the further education library, *Educ.Libr.Bull.* (Autumn 1977), 20 – 28
3 Pearce B. L., Libraries in English Further Education, 1926 – 1976, *MA Dissertation,* University College, London, 1976 (pp. 125 – 39 based on survey of existing tertiary college libraries)
4 *Recommended Salaries and Conditions of Service for Non-university Academic Library Staff, 1979/80* (London, Library Association, Jul. 1979)
5 NATFHE Conference resolutions reported in *NATFHE Journal* (Aug./Sep. 1979), 21
6 *'College Libraries: Recommended Standards of Library Provision in . . . Establishments of Further Education',* 2nd edn revised (London, Library Association, 1971)

INDEX